THE ANXIOUS ATTACHMENT RECOVERY WORKBOOK

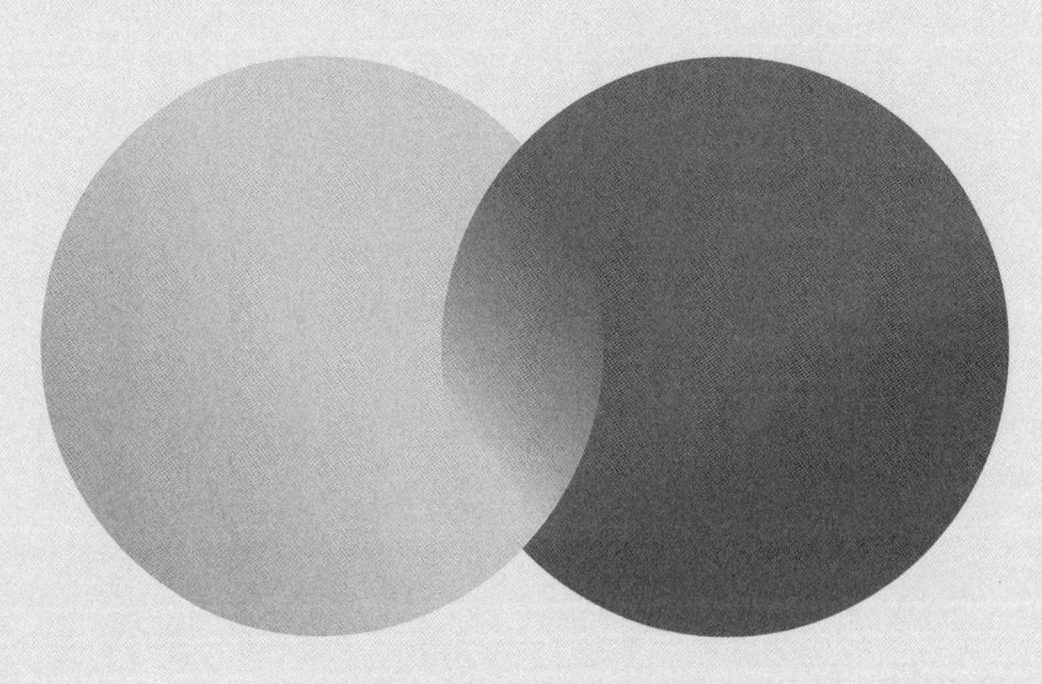

The ANXIOUS ATTACHMENT RECOVERY WORKBOOK

How to Develop Secure and Lasting Relationships

JESSICA DA SILVA, LMFT

an imprint of Sourcebooks

Cover Designer: Joshua R. Moore
Illustrations © undefined undefined/iStock/Getty Images: vi; © Ron Dale/iStock/Getty Images: x, throughout; © shima rasouli/iStock/Getty Images: 2, throughout; © Kolonko/iStock/Getty Images: 48 (masks); © Liubov Kondrateva/iStock/Getty Images: 67; © Dudi Mahpudi/iStock/Getty Images: 93; © dityazemli/Shutterstock: 96; © ai_yoshi/iStock/Getty Images: 97; © Montoo Gharial/Shutterstock: 100; © Tanya St/iStock/Getty Images: 116; © Leontura/Digital Vision Vectors/Getty Images: 125 (figure with roots); © azatvaleev/iStock/Getty Images: 138; © StarLineArts/iStock/Getty Images: 147; © undefined/iStock/Getty Images: 152; © ass29/iStock/Getty Images: 159; © Irina Kryvets/Shutterstock: 173
Author photo courtesy of Julianna Prebanda
Art Director: Lisa Schreiber
Art Producer: Stacey Stambaugh
Editor: Safon Floyd
Production Editor: Rachel Taenzler
Production Designer: Jeffrey Piekarz

Published by Callisto Publishing LLC C/O Sourcebooks LLC
P.O. Box 4410, Naperville, Illinois 60567-4410
(630) 961-3900
callistopublishing.com

Printed and bound in the United States of America.
VP 10 9 8 7 6 5 4 3 2 1

CONTENTS

INTRODUCTION

Welcome! My name is Jessica Da Silva, and I'm a licensed mental health therapist and attachment coach helping adults end unhealthy attachment patterns, reconnect to their authentic selves, and build lasting confidence in their relationships.

This workbook was created for those who over-give, overthink, and hold on too tightly to love and relationships. While this workbook primarily speaks to romantic relationship dynamics, the concepts and tools can be broadly applied to all types of relationships. Within these pages, you'll explore how people with an anxious attachment style often act like open wells—pouring into others to quench their needs but feeling drained when their own cup is left empty. Despite their efforts and hopes for a different outcome, they often find themselves stuck in the same familiar story, feeling depleted, unloved, unsupported, and unimportant.

I remember being in a similar position years ago, where I couldn't see myself existing in any other way. I suffered from low self-esteem, poor emotional regulation, people-pleasing, self-neglect, extreme jealousy, and chronic worry, while pushing healthy love away and pursuing the hearts of those who were emotionally unavailable. This pattern was typical in my maternal lineage, as the women before me operated similarly.

If you can relate, I am here to tell you that just because this pain is all you know, it doesn't mean it has to be your life story. It most certainly doesn't mean you are predestined for a life of loneliness and dissatisfaction.

Learning about your attachment style can be transformative. Attachment theory explains how our early relationships shape the ways we connect, trust, and respond to intimacy in adulthood. Whether you operate from an anxious, avoidant, disorganized, or secure attachment style, understanding these patterns can help you recognize how they influence your behaviors in relationships. Overall, this awareness empowers you to make intentional decisions and shift from a cycle of depletion to relationships where you feel valued, supported, and truly connected.

While this book will provide tools to help you cultivate greater self-compassion, develop stronger emotional resilience, and create the fulfilling connections you deserve, it's not a substitute for therapy, medication, or medical treatment. Seeking a medical professional is nothing to be ashamed of, and it can help you address ongoing or severe emotional experiences.

Through my studies in psychology, postgraduate training in marriage and family therapy, and nearly a decade of working with individuals, couples, and families on relationship dynamics, one thing is clear: our early attachment experiences profoundly influence how we navigate our relationships today. By recognizing these patterns and learning tools to address relationship challenges, anyone who is motivated and willing can work toward earning a secure attachment and experiencing love in healthier, more fulfilling ways. This book will guide you on the right path!

Remember, growth is a process, and while shifting your relationship patterns can be challenging at times, every small step forward brings you closer to the relationships you truly desire.

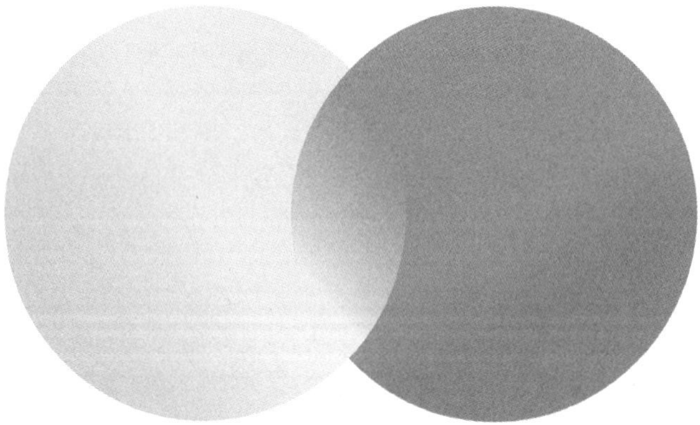

HOW TO USE THIS BOOK

You'll find two main sections in this workbook. In part one of the workbook, you will learn the foundations of attachment theory and the anxious attachment style, including the patterns of thought, feeling, and behavior that have shaped your relationships and their origins.

In parts two and three, you will dive deeper into the workbook exercises and tools for processing, managing, and healing your anxious attachment style to achieve and sustain a more authentic and empowered version of yourself. Whether you work through this book independently or with a therapist, use the information and exercises from start to finish as the exercises build upon each other. Therapists may use this book to guide sessions or recommend it as "homework," while patients can use it independently or alongside professional support.

As you work through this workbook, remember to be patient with yourself. Healing and growth are not linear, and it's okay if you fall behind or can't commit to working on it consistently. Take it at your own pace—this journey is about doing what you can and learning along the way. Celebrate small victories and give yourself grace when things feel difficult. Seeking additional support through coaching or therapy can be helpful in processing and integrating the information into your life. As you complete the exercises, assess where you may need more guidance and support.

My hope is that you use this workbook as a guide to navigate your way toward secure attachment and building healthier, more fulfilling relationships.

PART I

UNDERSTANDING ATTACHMENT THEORY

Before we dive into the strategies for developing secure attachment, it's important that you first learn about how you arrived at your current relationship circumstances. This means understanding the experiences that shaped how you approach love, trust, and connection.

According to attachment science, your strategies for coping with relational distress result from deeply ingrained attachment patterns that were formed in response to early relationships, particularly with primary caregivers; however, these strategies can be influenced by other attachment figures throughout your life. These patterns influence how you interpret and react to perceived threats in close relationships, such as fears of abandonment, rejection, or not being loved the way you desire or need. With this knowledge, you can begin to make sense of why you keep re-creating similar relationship dynamics and can break free from repeating cycles that hinder you from experiencing more fulfilling connections.

By getting a comprehensive understanding of all the attachment styles, you will learn how you may exhibit traits of more than one attachment style and be better able to identify how other people experience connection, which can be helpful in debunking the idea that we all experience love in the same way. Recognizing these patterns is the first step to transforming them.

CHAPTER 1

WHAT ARE ATTACHMENT STYLES?

"If we value our relationships, we must be willing to examine the ways our past experiences shape our expectations of others." —John Bowlby

It's important to understand how our lived experiences shape us and impact our approaches to love, trust, and connection. Once we have a greater understanding of our experiences and selves, we will be able to learn and apply new strategies for developing more secure attachments.

Keep in mind that your reactions, whether subtle or intense, are linked to deeper emotional wounds and past experiences.

By developing a comprehensive understanding of all the attachment styles, you will learn how you may exhibit traits of more than one. You'll be better able to identify how others experience connection, which can be helpful in understanding that we all experience love in different ways.

Why Do I Keep Going After the Same Emotionally Unavailable People?

Natasha was a highly motivated woman. She was a single mom working as a nurse at a local hospital and wanting to create a happy, healthy home for herself and her family. She was intelligent, kind, and eager to break her cycle of dating emotionally unavailable men, as they never made her feel truly valued or supported.

She came to me, as most people do, through learning about her attachment style from one of my social media posts and was determined to end the dysfunctional relationship patterns she was experiencing. Though she hated feeling insignificant and undervalued in her relationships, she couldn't understand why she kept attracting (and being attracted to) these specific individuals. She found herself over-functioning, over-giving, and overdoing in all her relationships, feeling disappointed that her loving actions weren't reciprocated. Instead, she was made to feel like she was "too needy" and "too much" for those she partnered with. These accusations made her feel worse about herself, solidifying her belief that she was a burden to others. "If this belief isn't true, then why has everyone in my life made me feel like I'm too much or too needy?"

By understanding her attachment style, she could more clearly see where her strong emotional reactions came from, why she tended to over-give in relationships, and why she kept looking for the same type of love interest to re-create these familiar relationship patterns.

It wasn't that she was attracting all the same types of people, but rather, that she was choosing to commit to these individuals due to underlying familiar patterns of experiencing relationships. These unhealthy ways of experiencing love were all that she knew, and by understanding these patterns, she was able to make wiser, healthier choices in her relationships moving forward.

What Is Attachment Theory?

Attachment theory provides a valuable shortcut to understanding how we form and maintain close relationships. This psychological approach, pioneered by John Bowlby and later conceptualized by Mary Ainsworth through her groundbreaking Strange Situation experiment, is one of the most revealing in the field, as it explores how caregivers and their children relate to one another. Ainsworth's observations of how children reacted when their caregiver left them with a stranger in a controlled room unveiled patterns in attachment styles, shedding light on the dynamics of relationships, such as how early interactions with caregivers shape a child's sense of security, trust, and emotional regulation.

Ainsworth observed three different ways that a child relates to their caregiver, which she called "attachment styles." These styles include secure, anxious ambivalent (or preoccupied), and avoidant (or dismissive avoidant).

In the experiment, children with secure attachment were distressed when their caregiver left but could eventually calm down and interact with the stranger. Once their caregiver returned, they were content to seek comfort from them and easily soothed.

Anxious children were highly distressed by the separation and had difficulty being comforted by the stranger, often exhibiting a lot of caution and guardedness. When their caregiver returned, they appeared ambivalent, wanting to be close to their caregiver while also pushing them away with anger and frustration.

Avoidant attached children showed little distress during separation from their caregiver and were indifferent to the stranger in the room. When the caregiver returned, the child avoided or ignored them.

In later studies by Mary Main, a fourth attachment style was discovered, the disorganized (or fearful avoidant) attachment style. In these cases, when the caregiver left, the child was often apprehensive about the stranger, and when the caregiver returned, the child appeared confused and fearful.

These studies highlighted how our earliest interactions with caregivers greatly influence how we relate to others and perceive love, trust, and security in relationships.

Researchers Cindy Hazan and Phillip Shaver later discovered that we carry these styles of relating into our adult relationships. This gives us a framework to understand why humans think, feel, and behave the way we do regarding love and connection, whether with romantic partners, friends, family members, or colleagues. By learning healthier strategies for navigating relational stress, we can learn to shift from insecure to secure attachment.

The Anxious Attachment Style

People with an anxious attachment style, like Natasha in the case study on page 4, tend to repeat relationship dynamics resembling those created with their earliest attachment figures, where they continue to feel worried, insignificant, doubtful, and needy.

Similar to Sigmund Freud's "repetition compulsion" theory, we unconsciously re-create past relationship experiences, despite how painful or unsatisfying they are, hoping to resolve unprocessed traumas and unresolved conflicts. Without awareness, we remain stuck in unfulfilling patterns, prompting many to seek professional support to break the cycles that have plagued their relationships and emotional well-being for so long.

Historically, at least one caregiver of individuals with an anxious attachment style offered inconsistent and unpredictable caregiving. This was observed and noted by Ainsworth in the Strange Situation experiment discussed earlier. Ainsworth also observed that some mothers quickly shifted from calm to chaotic in their parenting style. They were loving parents with good intentions but had difficulty meeting their children's needs in an attuned and consistent way. Ainsworth noted that as their children became more frustrated due to the lack of proper support, mothers became irritated and even hostile toward them.

A typical example of this situation in real time is when a parent is working and the child wants some form of attention; the parent responds calmly at first, but as the child continues to probe, the parent's anxiety spikes and they raise their voice or show frustration, saying things like "I can't focus with you interrupting me!" or "I don't have time for this." The child then feels like an inconvenience, leading them to believe they are "too much" or "too needy" and question what they can expect from those they rely on.

In other cases, parents may resort to physical violence to try to regain control or release the intense stress they feel in response to their child's behavior. Both subtle and more extreme forms of abandonment and rejection not only harm the child emotionally and physically but also create an "insecure child-parent bond," instilling unease instead of trust and security. This apprehension causes anxiously attached children to resort to more indirect or manipulative ways of meeting their needs, such as passive aggression, withholding love, and excessive bids for connection, which we will discuss further in chapter 2.

If not addressed, these faulty belief systems and unhealthy ways of meeting their needs will be replicated in their future relationships, thus perpetuating cycles of insecurity, emotional distance, and difficulty forming healthy, trusting connections.

The Avoidant Attachment Style

On the opposite side of the insecure attachment spectrum, individuals with an avoidant (or dismissive avoidant) attachment style have learned through consistent emotional unavailability or unresponsive caregiving that it is safer to suppress emotional needs than to risk the pain of rejection and disappointment. Many assume that people with an avoidant attachment don't experience anxiety due to their reserved and cool appearance. However, Bowlby characterized avoidant attachment as part of the anxious category because, despite appearing indifferent or self-reliant, avoidantly attached individuals still experienced heightened stress regarding threats to their attachment bonds.

In his view, avoidant attachment behaviors are protective responses to the fear of rejection or emotional unavailability from attachment figures.

In the Strange Situation experiment, Ainsworth observed that mothers of avoidant children were unaffectionate, commanding, insulting, rejecting, and less emotionally expressive. To cope with the pain of not getting their emotional needs met, avoidant children emotionally cut off or distanced themselves from their internal experiences. They would achieve this "emotional cut-off" by engaging in activities and distracting themselves to avoid confronting deeper feelings or emotional needs. Based on their experiences, avoidant attached individuals believe it's safer to rely only on themselves and to keep their feelings hidden from others.

A typical example of avoidant parenting in real-time is a caregiver who highly values self-sufficiency and thus tells their child to "toughen up" or "do it on your own" when the child is looking for support. This constant dismissal of emotional needs teaches the child, over time, to avoid seeking support in moments when they might feel they need it, and instead handle their emotions alone.

More subtle forms of avoidant parenting are when parents are experiencing their own mental health issues and unresolved traumas that impede their ability to be emotionally present and available to their children. When a parent is struggling with depression, for example, they may appear unresponsive, distant, and checked out, making the child feel ignored, insignificant, and as though they have to handle their emotions independently.

This style of relating to themselves and others becomes their default approach in relationships, making it challenging for them to trust others fully or feel comfortable relying on anyone for emotional support. As you can imagine or may know from firsthand experience, these more detached and unresponsive ways of engaging and addressing emotional needs can cause much of the conflict and disconnect they experience with others who may need more from them.

The Disorganized Attachment Style

Disorganized attachment (disorganized/disoriented or fearful-avoidant attachment) can be a bit more complicated to understand than other attachment styles because people with this orientation exhibit a combination of anxious and avoidant tendencies. In other words, they don't have a consistent strategy for coping with relational stress, as they will unpredictably seek closeness and intimacy like anxious attachments while simultaneously pushing others away or acting distant like avoidant attachments.

Continuing Ainsworth's efforts in studying parent-child bonding, researcher Mary Main identified a pattern in some children that didn't fit into the existing attachment classifications (secure, anxious, or avoidant). These children sought closeness to their caregivers in contradictory or disoriented ways, such as moving closer to them and freezing in the middle of the room, dissociating, or acting confused. Hence the name "disorganized attachment."

Main discovered that the parents of these children were abusive and frightening and suffered tragic early losses that they never fully grieved or processed. These behaviors caused the children to become fearful and anxious about being able to safely depend on their caregivers to meet their emotional needs.

It's important to note that the internal conflict and behavioral manifestations of disorganized individuals are expressed and experienced differently than those who may flip-flop between both anxious and avoidant tendencies due to different styles of relating with more than one attachment figure. For instance, someone with a disorganized attachment style might get angry at their partner for not caring about them but will be confused about whether they need closeness or distance in that moment. Meanwhile, someone with a mix of anxious and avoidant tendencies may have more clarity about their need for reassurance or space from the situation.

Disorganized attachment can result from different parenting behaviors, but the underlying common denominator is that the child experiences confusion and fear with their attachment figure, which creates an inconsistent way of coping with their distress or anxiety. For example, if the parent is sometimes physically or emotionally abusive but sometimes loving, the child may see their caregiver as a source of fear and also a source of safety. More subtle factors could include growing up in environments that are extremely unstable and even dangerous, where they witness violence, addiction, manipulation, poverty, and other circumstances that create a sense of constant threat.

In adulthood, these individuals may have a hard time understanding what they need or want in a relationship and seek out partners who exhibit similar hurtful and confusing behaviors.

The Secure Attachment Style

In contrast to insecure attachment styles, people with a secure attachment style tend to have a positive and trusting perspective on themselves and their relationships. They are comfortable with intimacy and can give and receive love in balanced ways. Luckily for us, they can serve as a model for how healthy and fulfilling connections can look.

According to Ainsworth in her Strange Situation experiment, children with secure attachments felt comfortable exploring their environment. They exhibited signs of both dependence—looking back at their caregiver when they went off to play with toys—and independence: when their mother left the room, they were able to move on from their distress confidently, knowing that their caregiver would soon return. When their caregiver returned, they were eager to see them and were quickly soothed and comforted by their presence. Later research by

Alan Sroufe indicated that securely attached individuals developed positive expectations in their home environment, which translated into positive experiences in social settings and higher resiliency, self-esteem, empathy, independence, and emotional well-being.

Parents of securely attached children are generally emotionally responsive, available, attuned to their child's needs, encouraging, and reliable. This "secure base," as Bowlby calls it, allows children to take risks, grow, face challenges, and become autonomous individuals who can safely rely on the people around them.

The good news is that parents don't have to be perfect to raise securely attached humans. That's an entirely unrealistic expectation and a recipe for shame and guilt. Instead, they should strive to be "good enough," showing attentiveness and responsiveness most of the time. It's also important to note that having a secure base with one attachment figure is sufficient. Bowlby emphasized the power of having experienced a secure bond with even one supportive figure, whether a parent, caregiver, or mentor, and how it can positively impact a person's ability to form secure attachments in later relationships. In his book *Secure Base,* he explains that a secure connection can provide a model for future relationships, even if someone's early environment was generally difficult or unstable. Simply by understanding that a more stable connection is possible, we can begin to strive for and seek that stability in our lives.

Not only did these findings bring relief to my own life, but they continue to comfort those I share this knowledge with, as it highlights the power of knowing that something more loving and fulfilling exists beyond the relational pain we've endured. This awareness opens the door to healing, inspiring hope that we can cultivate healthier, more secure relationships in our own lives.

Styles May Vary

It's important to note that attachment styles fall on a spectrum and that, in most cases, we tend to resonate with more than one style. Though at first glance this might seem confusing, this multidimensionality is a result of the many interactions and close relationships we've been exposed to throughout our lives, thus influencing the way we view and experience ourselves and others when it comes to connection.

This explains why you may notice yourself engaging in a specific attachment style with some people and another with others. It's also why you may exhibit different coping strategies in different circumstances. For example, perhaps you find yourself more anxious with avoidant individuals and more avoidant with anxious individuals. Not only are these responses completely natural to human interaction, but your own attachment system can be triggered by various behaviors you find to be "safe" or "unsafe" given your past experiences.

Attachment styles are also not fixed and can fluctuate throughout our lives as we experience different relationships and significant life events. Bowlby emphasized that though our mental "working models" for relationships—in other words, our ideas and expectations of ourselves and others—become more solidified as we grow older, by being self-reflective and flexible in our perspectives, we can shift from insecure to secure ways of relating. Take heart in the knowledge that we have the power to reshape ourselves.

Attachment Style Interactions

Since each attachment style has distinct ways of experiencing relationships, it's no surprise that interactions vary between different attachment pairings. This is seen quite clearly in Sroufe's research where he grouped children with every combination of secure, avoidant, and anxious and observed their interactions.

Overall, children with secure attachments exhibited healthy interactions with every attachment style, meaning they were sensitive, attuned, collaborative, and engaging with all their peers. Avoidant children faced the most difficulty forming positive connections, as they were more reserved or exhibited defiant and hurtful behaviors. Children with anxious attachments sought connection with their peers but had trouble with healthy collaboration and emotional regulation.

Longitudinal studies also discovered that these styles of interacting persist, which explains why we see similar attachment dynamic interactions among adults. For example, pairings of individuals who both have secure attachment styles tend to experience more stability in their adult relationship dynamics. They are often empathetic and supportive, exhibit good communication and conflict-resolution skills, and are flexible with meeting each other's needs.

Secure and anxious pairings can face challenges due to the anxious partner's impulsiveness but often build a healthier bond, as the anxious partner is open to the secure partner's support.

Secure and avoidant attachment dynamics can also encounter difficulties, as avoidants can have trouble collaborating more constructively and kindly. However, as studies show, with encouragement and flexibility, secure attachments can help them open up and cultivate trust.

Though pairings with two anxious individuals may be able to connect more deeply, they can struggle with creating a stable foundation, as they have difficulties with self-regulation, collaboration, and conflict-resolution skills.

Anxious and avoidant pairings face challenges due to a push-pull dynamic: the anxious partner seeks closeness, while the avoidant partner feels overwhelmed and withdraws to regain independence.

Pairings with two avoidant individuals may appear harmonious, but these relationships often have a more transactional feel, as each partner tends to prioritize independence and emotional self-sufficiency over intimacy.

Those with disorganized attachment may unpredictably fluctuate between their avoidant and anxious tendencies depending on how avoidant or anxious their partner behaves.

Attachment Style Grid

ANXIOUS ATTACHMENT STYLE

CAUSES	SYMPTOMS
Inconsistent and unpredictable caregiving or support	Worry and fear about not getting needs met; feeling needy, hypervigilant, and distrusting
Lack of boundaries / enmeshment	People-pleasing, lack of self-trust or self-knowing, codependency, self-neglect
Emotional instability	Hypervigilance, anxiety, walking on eggshells
Rejection	Heightened need for closeness, reassurance, and validation
Loss or abandonment	Hyper-fixated on inconsistencies and disconnection

AVOIDANT ATTACHMENT STYLE

CAUSES	SYMPTOMS
Emotional unavailability	Suppression of needs, hyper-independence; more logic based and intellectualizes emotional experiences
Criticism	Perfectionism, fear of disapproval, shame, not ever feeling good enough, over-compensating behaviors
Dismissal	Belief feelings are unimportant and feel insignificant or misunderstood
Neglect	Self-reliant and feels as though no one will meet their needs
Intrusive behavior	Desire for freedom, space, and privacy
Demanding behavior	Desire for respect and individuality

CONTINUED >

CONTINUED FROM THE PREVIOUS PAGE

DISORGANIZED ATTACHMENT STYLE

CAUSES	SYMPTOMS
Abusive, threatening, or frightening behavior	Fearful of attachment figures and often views them as the "enemy"; feels on edge or on guard, distrustful
Neglect	Feels alone, unsupported, and insignificant
Emotional instability	Hypervigilance, anxiety, and walking on eggshells
Reverse roles of parent-child dynamic	Parentification and codependency; lack of boundaries or sense of individual self
Unresolved trauma	Belief that their caregivers' projections about themselves are true
Chaotic environments	Chronic stress, confusion, inability to stay present

SECURE ATTACHMENT STYLE

CAUSES	SYMPTOMS
Affection	Comfortable seeking physical or emotional proximity
Attentiveness	Feels seen, cared for, significant; high self-esteem
Responsiveness	Trusts that their needs will get met
Reliability	Knows they can depend on their attachment figures
Predictability	Emotional stability and peace of mind; can take risks; autonomous, resilient
Empathy	Able to accept their emotions and internal experiences; good social skills
Warmth	Kind and sensitive with oneself and others
Healthy boundaries	Can assert needs and has a sense of self
Emotional stability	Can self-regulate and co-regulate

Key Takeaways

Hopefully, this chapter helped you better understand attachment theory, the different styles of relating, where they stem from, and how they may influence your relationships. As you've discovered, our earliest childhood experiences play a pivotal role in how we think, feel, and behave today. These mental "working models," as Bowlby calls them, have become the representations and expectations of how we perceive ourselves, others, and relationships.

Though these models become more ingrained in how we operate as we age, through awareness and implementing healthier ways to respond to our insecurities, we can break the painful and self-sabotaging patterns that have been running our lives for generations. In the upcoming chapters, you will learn just how to do this!

- People with an anxious attachment style often re-create relationship dynamics that mirror their earliest attachment experiences, leading them to feel worried, unimportant, uncertain, and overly dependent.
- Avoidant attachment develops when consistent emotional unavailability or unresponsive caregiving leads individuals to believe suppressing their needs is safer than risking rejection or disappointment.
- Disorganized attachment is more complex because it combines anxious and avoidant tendencies, with individuals unpredictably seeking closeness while also pushing others away.
- Individuals with secure attachment view themselves and their relationships positively, feeling comfortable with intimacy and able to give and receive love in a balanced way.
- Attachment styles exist on a spectrum and can change over time based on relationships and life experiences. Each attachment style experiences relationships differently, so interactions vary across attachment pairings.

CHAPTER 2

UNDERSTANDING YOUR ANXIOUS ATTACHMENT STYLE

"Every thought we think is creating our future. Each one of us creates our experiences by our thoughts and our feelings." —Louise L. Hay

Now that you have a better understanding of attachment theory and insight into how you may relate to others, we are going to take a closer look at the anxious attachment style—which is probably what drew you to this book!

In this chapter, we will begin to uncover how your anxious attachment style impacts your day-to-day interactions and behaviors. Research studies indicate that our attachment style influences not only how we navigate relationships but also how we approach life's challenges. As you know from the previous chapter, your intense reactions aren't just coming from nowhere—they are derived from your previous experiences. These reactions, though often uncomfortable, can give you great insight into the parts of yourself that need attention and healing.

We will reframe the way you look at your challenges with jealousy, neediness, people-pleasing, rumination, lack of boundaries, negative self-view, and fear of abandonment so that you can begin to quiet the harsh inner critic that has been making you believe that you are "damaged," "crazy," "too much," "too needy," or "difficult to love." This insight and newfound awareness will help you shift from feeling like a victim to becoming an empowered author of your own life.

When Relationships Trigger Self-Doubt

"I hate that I turn into this needy person in relationships… As soon as I'm remotely interested in someone, my insecurities go from 0 to 100!" Kyle, a divorced male in his late forties, was seeking help to address his relationship-sabotaging behaviors. Though confident at work and in his business matters, he couldn't understand why he felt so insecure when it came to love, often becoming more agreeable, submissive, and self-conscious around his love interest. He would even find himself making up stories to appear more attractive, such as exaggerating his income or workout frequency. He felt embarrassed about being dishonest but wanted to make a good impression. When I asked him why he couldn't be his true self on dates, he paused and said, "Because I don't see my true self as good enough." As we began to unpack the underlying motives urging him to appear "cooler" or "more appealing" than he believed himself to be, he learned that he had nothing to lose and everything to gain by being his most authentic self. The impulse to be someone he wasn't arose from his fears of abandonment and rejection. He believed that if he could do more or be more, this would compensate for his perceived shortcomings and therefore others wouldn't leave him. Though this strategy may have worked in the short term, it was not sustainable because, eventually, the facade dissolves, and you are left facing the same unresolved feelings and unmet needs that were there all along.

The Root of Your Anxious Attachment

Like many others, Kyle, who has a predominantly anxious attachment style, faces the common challenges of overcompensating for perceived flaws or lack of self-worth. This can manifest as over-giving, people-pleasing, self-sacrificing, suppressing one's own needs, and over-attuning to the feelings and needs of others. The problem is that these behaviors not only minimize our needs, but they can also appear disingenuous and overbearing to others.

I saw this behavior manifest in my relationship with my own mother, where she over-extended herself to ensure her loved ones were happy but exhibited resentment when others did not give in the same way or value her efforts as she expected. Her deep dissatisfaction with others, especially my two sisters and me, would make us feel like we were the most awful and ungrateful people, which forced us to become people pleasers to ensure her contentment and a peaceful home environment. Not only was my mother over-giving to meet her emotional needs for validation and belonging, but due to our fear of abandonment and rejection, we, too, behaved in disingenuous ways to meet our emotional needs for acceptance and love. And so the cycle continues, where we reenact these same relationship patterns with those we love in our efforts to feel loved and avoid abandonment but create resentment and emotional exhaustion in the process. This pattern, driven by unmet needs and fears, can lead to the very disconnection we're trying to avoid, trapping us in a loop of seeking closeness while pushing it further away.

These more exaggerated and self-neglecting behaviors in relationships, or even when merely interested in someone, stem from a deep fear of abandonment. As discussed in chapter 1, people with an anxious attachment style experienced a lot of inconsistency and unpredictability with their earliest attachment figures, which can be perceived as abandonment. We often think of abandonment in the form of physical neglect, but it is also expressed as emotional neglect, which can be equally damaging. Emotional neglect is when someone is not meeting your needs, not respecting your boundaries, not keeping their word, and not valuing your presence or what you contribute to the relationship. Therefore, it's about people who fail to show up for you not just physically but also emotionally and mentally.

When people behave in these inconsistent or neglectful ways, our attachment system becomes hyperactivated, and we resort to unhealthy attachment behaviors to ensure our safety and security.

How to Know When You're Anxiously Attached

Having an anxious attachment style can affect your thoughts, emotions, and physical sensations, which amplifies fears of rejection or abandonment. Understanding these patterns is the first step to breaking them. In your mind, it may appear as cognitive distortions like catastrophizing, personalization, or black-and-white thinking. In your body, it might manifest as tension, restlessness, or physical discomfort when emotional security feels threatened. By identifying these signs and understanding what's driving them, you can respond proactively, address unmet needs, and navigate your relationship insecurities in healthier ways. This awareness is key to transforming attachment patterns and feeling more secure within yourself and your relationships.

Anxious in the Mind

People with an anxious attachment style have many fearful thinking patterns when it comes to close relationships that are typically rooted in a fear of abandonment or rejection. It's as if they jump to worst-case scenarios, often amplifying what they're experiencing. In psychology, these automatic negative thought patterns are called cognitive distortions because they reinforce insecurities and skew perception.

Common cognitive distortions in anxious attachment include:

- **Catastrophizing:** Assuming the worst-case scenario in relationships
- **Personalization:** Believing someone's mood or reaction is caused by you and feeling responsible for it
- **Black-and-White Thinking:** Viewing the relationship as either perfect or completely falling apart
- **"Should" Statements:** Holding rigid expectations about how others should act and feeling disappointed when they don't
- **Discounting the Positive:** Minimizing good experiences while focusing on what's lacking

Another key aspect of anxious attachment is recognizing protest behaviors: actions triggered when emotional security feels threatened. Coined by Mary Ainsworth and expanded on by Amir Levine and Rachel Heller in their book *Attached*, these behaviors are attempts to restore connection but often lead to complications in adult relationships.

Common protest behaviors include:

- Repeatedly texting or calling
- Seeking excessive reassurance
- Passive aggressiveness or silent treatment
- Jealousy, possessiveness, or testing the relationship
- Angry outbursts or conflict-seeking
- People-pleasing and over-explaining

Anxious in the Body

Anxious attachment isn't just in your mind; it shows up in your body as well. Physical signs of anxious attachment might include a racing heart, restlessness, tension, or even feeling a sense of panic when you feel disconnected from a partner or loved one. You might notice shallow breathing, sweating, trouble concentrating, or stomach discomfort when anticipating rejection or conflict. For some, this can escalate to insomnia, fatigue, or even physical aches.

As you will learn later in this book, it's important to pay attention to how you are feeling because these sensations are signals from your nervous system indicating what you may need in order to regain balance and a sense of safety. Ignoring or suppressing these feelings can amplify distress, whereas recognizing and addressing them allows you to respond proactively. For example, if you notice tension in your chest or a knot in your stomach, it may signal a need for connection or reassurance—or it may highlight an unmet emotional need within yourself.

Understanding and addressing these physical responses is a crucial step toward breaking anxious attachment patterns and cultivating inner peace and healthier relationships.

Identify Triggers

Unlike stress that is a response to present challenges, a trigger activates a reaction rooted in past emotional experiences that is often disproportionate to what is actually happening in the moment.

Cognitive behavioral therapy (CBT) can be useful in helping people with anxious attachments become aware of their triggers by bringing attention to unhelpful thoughts and behaviors, as well as the body's physical responses to emotional distress, such as fight, flight, freeze, or fawn coping mechanisms. By incorporating somatic experiencing, such as tuning into bodily sensations, you can more quickly identify when you're triggered. For example:

In fight mode, you may experience muscle tension, a faster heart rate, and a surge of adrenaline.

In flight mode, you might feel restlessness, shallow breathing, and have a strong desire to leave or escape the situation.

In freeze mode, you might feel numbness, heaviness, or an inability to speak or move.

In fawn mode, you may experience a racing heart or shallow breathing while simultaneously trying to maintain a calm or agreeable demeanor.

Begin assessing your triggers by reflecting on past experiences in which you noticed your body engaging in one of these modes.

What in that moment caused you to become distressed? This could be a place, sound, smell, sight, sensation, situation, memory, thought, emotion, etc. Example: My partner hasn't returned my call.

What thoughts arose? Example: They are ignoring me.

How did those thoughts make you feel? Example: Worried and sad.

What action did you take? Example: I kept calling until they answered.

What past experience does this remind you of? Example: When my mother would leave for hours without calling or indicating when she'd return.

By becoming aware of our triggers and the patterns associated with them, we can begin to interrupt the cycle and choose more intentional responses, as we'll discuss later in the book.

How Anxious Attachment Impacts Self-Worth and Self-Esteem

As discussed in the previous chapter, studies have shown the impact of inconsistent and unpredictable caregiving on the development of the anxious attachment style. The repercussions of these behaviors on a more consistent basis can hurt our self-esteem, as we lack the confidence to trust ourselves and others. Self-esteem isn't something we are born with; it's cultivated through our beliefs and actions. If we've been directly or indirectly taught that we are "too much," "too needy," "too clingy," "too emotional," and "too overwhelming," for example, this will directly affect the way we feel and behave.

For example, suppose you believe you're too needy because your mother would often sigh or tell you to leave her alone when you approached her in moments of stress. As a result, you felt like a burden, which then caused you to suppress your emotions and needs and become more appeasing to others. The inconsistent and unpredictable manners in which our needs are met or unmet create a sense of insecurity and self-doubt that negatively impacts our self-esteem.

This is a stark contrast to people with a secure attachment style, as their caregivers were mostly consistent, attuned, predictable, and affirming. These experiences positively impacted their child's self-esteem and they developed the confidence to trust themselves and others. This confidence allowed them to communicate assertively, embrace their emotions and needs, take risks, honor their boundaries, and navigate challenges proactively.

Both examples show contrasting patterns of thinking, feeling, and behaving to our given circumstances. The first example, with anxious attachments, illustrates how consistently unattuned behaviors can cause us to feel insecure about ourselves and others. Conversely, with secure attachments, consistently attuned behaviors can cause us to feel confident about ourselves and others. These developed concepts of self and others influence our perceptions and interactions in every aspect of life. They shape how we interpret feedback, approach relationships, and respond to challenges. When self-esteem is low, we may misinterpret others' intentions, doubt our capabilities, or expect rejection. Conversely, a positive self-concept allows us to approach life with a sense of worthiness, resilience, and trust in our abilities, setting a foundation for healthier relationships and personal growth.

The good news is that self-esteem is not available for some and not others. With effort and the right support, anyone can build a healthier sense of self-worth, regardless of past experiences or challenges.

How Anxious Attachment Impacts Relationships

Anxious attachment often impacts relationships in profound ways, creating cycles of emotional distress and disconnection. Rooted in early life experiences, this attachment style creates insecurities that manifest through jealousy, neediness, difficulty with boundaries, and struggles with trust and vulnerability. People with anxious attachment may feel stuck in self-sabotaging behaviors like ruminating, overanalyzing, or people-pleasing, driven by a deep fear of abandonment. These patterns can create misunderstandings, break trust, and hinder intimacy. However, by identifying these behaviors and addressing the underlying fears, it's 100 percent possible to improve emotional regulation, respond differently to your attachment insecurities, and increase your sense of security in relationships.

Jealousy

Insecurities about your relationships can cause you to engage in counterproductive behaviors as you unintentionally push away the love you desire through your distrust and underlying fears. This isn't your fault—you were conditioned to be wary of love due to your past experiences. But without addressing these issues, you'll continue to sabotage the very love you crave.

One common way anxious attachments may sabotage their relationships is through jealousy and possessiveness. Jealousy often stems from fear of abandonment; when one fears losing something, they may cling more tightly. This behavior is similar to the fight response we may engage in to cope with a perceived threat we're experiencing in our environment. Let's say you notice your partner talking to someone more attractive, or that they choose to spend time with other people over you. Your attachment system may interpret that as a sign of danger, and to preserve the connection, you become angry, clingy, controlling, critical, over-analytical, or demanding of excessive reassurance and validation.

In addition, your low self-esteem, rooted in a lack of confidence and trust, adds fuel to your fears, as you may be operating from the familiar negative thought patterns around not being "good enough" or "lovable." As we touched on in the previous chapter, these thoughts influence your feelings and, therefore, the actions you take, which might be less than desirable.

Lack of Boundaries

Another way having an anxious attachment style may negatively impact relationships is by not respecting others' boundaries or struggling to establish one's own. This tendency often comes from *enmeshed family dynamics*, a psychological term for when people's boundaries are blurred or nonexistent. In enmeshed relationships, people become overly involved in each other's emotional lives, thoughts, and decisions, making it difficult to maintain a sense of independence and individuality. Without this sense of self or individuality, we don't know where we begin and others end, as we have difficulty identifying our identity, needs, emotions, values, desires, and limitations outside of someone else.

A lack of boundaries can manifest in various ways, such as saying "yes" when you genuinely want to say "no," pressuring someone to meet your needs when they are unwilling or unable to do so, taking on the emotional burdens or responsibilities of others, and believing that you must fix someone else's pain. This lack of boundaries not only causes personal burnout but can make others feel consumed, overwhelmed, frustrated, confused, guilty, and resentful. We know through studies that autonomy and individuality are core character traits in secure attached relationships, which foster a sense of personal agency and self-worth. Without them, we may struggle with codependence or loss of self-identity, which can hinder the development of healthy, balanced relationships.

Neediness

Neediness is one of the most common traits associated with an anxious attachment style. Unfortunately, this tendency is frequently misunderstood, as it stems from an underlying fear rather than being an inherent part of someone's identity. Labeling ourselves as a "needy person" makes it much harder to separate ourselves from the behavior, which can lead to increased shame and lower self-esteem.

According to Levine and Heller in *Attached*, "most people are only as needy as their unmet needs." This statement is pivotal in highlighting that our "neediness" is a natural response to experiencing a lack of emotional security or connection. It reframes neediness not as a flaw or weakness but as a signal of unmet needs for emotional attunement.

As studies have shown, people with an anxious attachment style tend to have general needs for closeness, attention, and reassurance. When met inconsistently and unpredictably, a heightened sensitivity to signs of disconnection or rejection develops, often resulting in clinginess or attempts to control the relationship dynamic to regain a sense of security. These behaviors can be sabotaging, as they can create tension or pressure on the relationship. The inconsistent fulfillment of these needs also creates a cycle of emotional dependency, making it difficult to trust that love and connection will remain stable without constant effort or proof.

Addressing these unmet needs, both individually and within the relationship, can foster a greater sense of stability and satisfaction.

Trouble with Trust and Vulnerability

When caregivers of those with anxious attachments alternated between being attentive and emotionally unavailable, it created uncertainty about whether their needs for love and security would be consistently met. This unpredictability fostered a sense of hypervigilance and worry in relationships, making it hard to trust others fully. These behaviors are expressed through the cognitive distortions or automatic negative thinking patterns they engage in, such as catastrophizing and discounting the positive. Rather than giving people the benefit of the doubt, they assume others will let them down.

Additionally, their self-worth often becomes tied to their relationships, leading to fears that being too vulnerable might drive others away or confirm their worst fear of rejection. These patterns make opening up to others challenging, even though they crave deeper intimacy. Rather than vulnerably sharing their feelings and needs, they may indirectly communicate by seeking constant reassurance, dropping hints, acting overly accommodating, or expressing their distress through criticism or passive-aggressive actions. These indirect ways of asking for attention or care help them avoid the risk of rejection but can cause confusion and frustration in relationships.

However, as I've learned from personal experience, being vulnerable helps you discover who is truly capable of supporting you and holding space for your feelings. You have nothing to lose and everything to gain by allowing yourself to be open and authentic.

People-pleasing

Because people with this attachment style have learned that being agreeable and accommodating meets their needs for validation and worth, anxious attachment and people-pleasing often go hand in hand.

Common people-pleasing behaviors include agreeing to unwanted commitments, over-apologizing, over-extending, being overly helpful, neglecting one's needs and desires to make others happy, and downplaying one's own feelings to avoid upsetting others.

People with an anxious attachment style often believe that putting their own needs and desires on the back burner and focusing on appeasing others will gain the approval they desire. This self-sacrificial behavior is a key aspect of their people-pleasing tendencies. When working with individuals who grapple with these behaviors, I've noticed that their tendency to neglect their needs in pursuit of external validation often leads to a disconnect from their authentic selves. They become so accustomed to serving others that they lose sight of their own feelings and desires. When they do reconnect with their innate experiences, they often struggle to believe that they are worthy of putting themselves first and may feel an overwhelming sense of guilt and shame when they do.

People-pleasing is a result of the enmeshment we've discussed. When we lack a sense of self or individuality, we seek validation from others to affirm our worth and sense of belonging. Breaking this pattern involves setting boundaries, building self-worth independent of others' approval, and allowing space for mutual needs.

Negative Self-view

Research done by Kim Bartholomew and Leonard Horowitz found that people with an anxious attachment style tend to view others as being more capable but view themselves as unworthy or flawed. This negative self-perception reinforces their low self-esteem and drives their excessive need for reassurance and approval from others to feel secure.

This negative self-view is expressed in various ways including frequently asking, "Do you really love me?" or, "Are you sure you want to be with me?" to feel secure in the relationship, not expressing needs from fear of being a burden or annoying, having a hard time accepting compliments or nice gestures, comparing themselves to others, feeling jealousy, and overcompensating to make up for their perceived flaws or shortcomings.

Another major behavior I see with anxious attachments who have a negative self-concept is pedestaling others. This can be dangerous because it overvalues the other person and undervalues themselves. By doing this, they also risk missing red flags or overlooking signs of incompatibility. When we put someone on a pedestal or idealize them, we stop seeing them as flawed, normal human beings like ourselves and instead view them as perfect or superior. This creates an imbalance in the relationship, making us feel unworthy or overly dependent on their approval.

Ruminating

People with an anxious attachment style ruminate—dwell on the same thoughts—as a form of coping with their distress. So much of the anxiety they experience stems from the uncertainties of life. Overthinking and overanalyzing create an illusion of control, and if they can anticipate what will happen, they can prevent themselves from experiencing possible pain.

The problem with rumination is that it's not always rooted in evidence or truth. Rather, it's perpetuated by more cognitive distortions such as mind reading—focusing on imagined beliefs that *They're annoyed with me* or *They think I'm annoying*—and future telling—thinking they know the future, such as, *They're going to leave me* or *They're going to find someone better than me.*

By ruminating, we build upon these stories in our minds, creating a distorted version of reality that often amplifies our fears and insecurities. This cycle reinforces negative beliefs, making it harder to see situations objectively and to break free from the anxiety tied to these thoughts.

In addition to the pain we inflict upon ourselves by rumination, we also project these stories onto those we love, assuming their thoughts, feelings, or intentions based on our fears rather than reality. This projection can lead to misunderstandings, unnecessary conflict, and a breakdown of trust in the relationship, as our loved ones may feel misunderstood or unfairly judged.

Fear of Abandonment

It is no surprise that the fear of abandonment is the common denominator of the sabotaging behaviors and pain we experience within ourselves and our relationships. It is this abandonment trauma that creeps into the way we think, feel, and behave, driving those fears of rejection, insecurity, and a constant need for reassurance. It shapes our attachment patterns and perpetuates our overthinking, overdependence, people-pleasing, loose boundaries, jealousy, emotional reactivity, and difficulty trusting others or ourselves.

People often feel confused when assessing where their abandonment issues come from, but as mentioned earlier, abandonment is not just being physically left or deserted. It can also stem from emotional neglect, inconsistent caregiving, or feeling unseen and unheard in important relationships. Even when a caregiver is physically present, if they are emotionally unavailable, critical, or unpredictable, it can create a sense of abandonment that deeply impacts a person's ability to trust and feel secure in relationships.

By assessing where your attachment wounds come from, you can begin to understand the origins of your behaviors. This insight is a critical piece in helping you see your triggers more objectively rather than personally, allowing you to respond to situations with greater self-awareness and emotional regulation. It empowers you to break unhealthy patterns, build healthier relationships, and cultivate a sense of security within yourself.

Key Takeaways

Understanding your anxious attachment style can be a liberating experience, as you now have the tools to recognize your patterns, identify your triggers, and take steps to respond more intentionally in relationships.

I can't tell you how many hundreds of messages I've received from people sharing their breakthroughs by simply recognizing their attachment style. This insight makes us feel less alone because it helps us understand that our struggles are part of a common and recognizable pattern shared by many others. It validates our feelings and experiences, showing that they stem from past circumstances rather than a personal defect.

Imagine the difference you can make within yourself and your relationships when you choose to respond differently to your triggers. Rather than automatically allowing your distortions and fears to lead you, you reclaim your power by learning to regulate your nervous system, reframe your thinking patterns, and choose healthier, secure responses.

Remember that you are not permanently stuck with your ways of experiencing love and relationships. We can change our "working models" or perceptions through self-reflection and intentional actions. By rewiring our attachment patterns, we can create new, more secure ways of thinking and relating to ourselves and others, fostering greater emotional stability and deeper connections. It does, however, require a consistent effort, like any skill we want to cultivate.

- Understanding the root of your attachment style can shed awareness on your patterns and help you make different choices that support the kind of relationships you want to experience.
- Your thoughts, feelings, and sensations can guide you to underlying emotional needs you may have to feel safe.
- Relationship insecurities can lead us to act in ways that unintentionally push away the love we crave due to fear and distrust.
- Meeting our needs can create more personal and relational stability.

"I can break unhealthy patterns to build healthier relationships."

PART II

HEALING YOUR ANXIOUS ATTACHMENT STYLE

Now that you have a better understanding of attachment theory and how you experience love and relationships, you can begin to take steps to break those patterns that have kept you in the same insecure and dissatisfying loop for so long. It is one thing to become aware of your challenges; it's an entirely different experience to actually do the work to change them. Awareness can be empowering, but it's just the beginning of the process. Without intentional steps toward change, awareness alone can trap us in cycles of overthinking, frustration, or self-blame. Change happens when we combine awareness with consistent action, patience, and self-compassion.

Each of the following sections will provide you with exercises, strategies, practices, and affirmations. These are not simply meant to be read but rather actively used in your journey to heal your anxious attachment style and grow more secure in relationships. You will learn how to address and move through your insecurities effectively and securely. The goal is to empower you to shift from insecure to secure ways of experiencing yourself and your romantic or platonic relationships, where connection feels stable, fulfilling, and rooted in mutual respect.

CHAPTER 3

ACCEPTING YOURSELF AND OTHERS

One of the most common requests I hear from those with an anxious attachment style is the desire to "fix" the parts that they hate about themselves. As with all insecure attachment styles, there is a deeply held sense of shame and belief around being unlovable, broken, inherently bad, or doomed. They are eager to eliminate their perceived imperfections and are not comfortable accepting these wounded parts of themselves. However, what we resist persists, and to heal and transform ourselves, we must stop resisting the darkness and instead embrace it as an essential part of the journey toward wholeness.

In this chapter, you will begin to courageously identify the tendencies in yourself you want to fix or eradicate and to implement evidence-based strategies to transform your relationship to them. By befriending our wounded parts with attention and grace, we compassionately quiet their cries for help and create a space where healing can occur. Instead of driving our actions from the shadows, these neglected parts feel seen and understood, allowing us to integrate them into our sense of self.

Through these practices and exercises, you will learn tools for releasing shame attached to your anxious attachment style and begin embracing yourself with compassion and understanding.

The Classic Anxious and Avoidant Struggle for Connection

Taylor and Brooke have been together for ten years and married for four. Looking for a more action-oriented approach to working through their triggers and disagreements, they sought my attachment coaching services to navigate their relationship challenges. Taylor had an anxious attachment style, and Brooke leaned more toward dismissive avoidant. They each loved the other but struggled to understand and communicate effectively, taking each other's bids for connection and need for space as personal attacks and a lack of mutual love. The more desperately Taylor sought reassurance and comfort from Brooke during moments of disconnection, the more Brooke shut down and pushed her away. Taylor was operating from the belief that she had to fight for her needs, whereas Brooke felt if he gave into Taylor's needs, he would lose his independence. This push-pull had been happening for years!

By understanding each other's attachment styles and differing needs, they could see each other's experience through a more objective lens rather than a personalized or defensive perspective. With this newfound sense of mutual acceptance, they were able to learn the tools to self-regulate, co-regulate, and communicate needs in proactive ways, and approach conflicts with empathy and curiosity rather than blame.

"When you change the way you look at things, the things you look at change."

– MAX PLANCK

Releasing Grudges

It's easy to blame our past and the people in it for our current circumstances. Though your experiences are entirely valid, if you don't let go of the grudge or resentment, you will continue to be a victim in your life rather than the empowered creator of your own story. Letting go doesn't mean forgetting or enabling what happened, it just means releasing its grip on your emotional well-being. By reflecting on your relationship with your attachment figures, you can see that their actions were shaped by their unresolved wounds, limitations, or circumstances rather than a reflection of your worth. This understanding allows you to separate their behavior from your identity, fostering compassion for both you and them.

Ask yourself the following questions:

How did my caregivers contribute to these beliefs?

What strengths or good intentions might they have had, even if they fell short in some areas?

What challenges or circumstances might my caregivers have been facing that affected their ability to love me in the way I needed?

How might my caregivers' own wounds or life circumstances have shaped them? What experiences from their childhood might have influenced their behavior?

What do I believe about love and relationships?

You have the power to rewrite your story by choosing to see it differently. Narrative therapy helps us let go of the past and reframe it in a way that is more supportive and conducive to the life and relationships we want to experience, by focusing on our strengths and goals. Through exploring and rewriting our narrative, we can transform the impact of past events on our present and future.

Rather than seeing your past as a hindrance, how can you rewrite your story to honor both your pain and the resilience you developed in response to your caregivers' limitations?

Identifying and Rewriting Your Anxious Attachment Beliefs

Your attachment style is linked to a belief system you learned from your earliest attachment figures about your worth, the reliability of others, and the nature of relationships. These beliefs, which are not inherently true, influence your emotions and behaviors, thus perpetuating your painful relationship experiences. By becoming aware of these dysfunctional patterns, you can replace your unhelpful beliefs with healthier, more supportive perspectives.

When are you most triggered in relationships? (Ex: when loved ones are unavailable or distant)

____

____

____

____

____

____

How do you apply their actions to your understanding of yourself? Consider "I am" statements (Ex: I am not important, worthy, or lovable.)

____

____

____

____

____

____

CONTINUED >

CONTINUED FROM THE PREVIOUS PAGE

How do these "I am" statements and beliefs make you feel, and where do they stem from in your past? (Ex: I feel angry and desperate. I felt this way when my mom didn't make time for me as a child.)

Are these "I am" statements and beliefs true about who you are, or do they result from your parents' personal limitations? (Ex: not true about who I really am)

How can you rewrite these beliefs to serve you better? (Ex: My parents' limitations do not define me. I am choosing to believe I am lovable and worthy.)

Recognizing Your Parents' Limitations to Cultivate Forgiveness

This visualization helps you see your parents as imperfect humans shaped by their experiences, fostering understanding and releasing resentment without excusing harmful behavior. You can listen to the guided visualization on my website at JessicaDaSilvaCoaching.com/resources.

---

1. Settle in:
   a. Find a quiet space.
   b. Sit or lie down with your eyes closed.
   c. Relax your body and take a few deep breaths.
2. Visualize your caregivers:
   a. Picture your caregivers as children and what they are wearing (looking at a photo can help).
   b. Picture them in their childhood environment—what kind of home, school, or family life they may have had.
   c. Notice their struggles, fears, and unmet needs.
3. See them as adults:
   a. Imagine them growing up and stepping into the role of caregivers but wearing the same clothes as they had in childhood, which symbolizes a stunt in their growth.
   b. Visualize them carrying their own unresolved wounds, insecurities, or limitations into parenthood.
4. Show compassion for their humanity:
   a. Repeat silently, "They are human just like me. I am learning to let go of my resentment" as often as you need.
5. Open your eyes when you are ready.

Attachment theory gives us a shortcut to understanding our attachment-related beliefs, the patterns they influence, and where they originate. Studies also indicate that these relationship patterns are carried into adulthood, which is why we find ourselves with different people yet feel similarly dissatisfied. These people may not be carbon copies of our earliest attachment figures, but they elicit the same emotions of abandonment and rejection we experienced in the past.

How could an understanding that my attachment tendencies come from my caregivers' limitations, and are not a direct reflection of who I am, help me to be more present in my current relationships?

Reworking Your Supportive Belief Systems in Current Relationships

By letting go of old, unhelpful belief systems, you can replace them with more empowering narratives that support the life and relationships you desire to experience. This exercise will help you become aware of how your old beliefs, and the behavioral patterns associated with them, may impact your relationships today. By implementing your new beliefs, you can evaluate whether your relationships align with your growth by observing how others respond to your changed behaviors and mindset.

When do you notice thoughts about not being good enough, being too needy, or being a burden in your current relationships? (Ex: in moments of distance and disconnect)

How do these thoughts make you feel? (Ex: worried and desperate)

CONTINUED >

CONTINUED FROM THE PREVIOUS PAGE

How do you behave? Think of protest behaviors. (Ex: pick fights, control, use silent treatment)

What are the consequences of these behaviors? (Ex: misunderstanding and more distance)

How do you want to behave instead? (Ex: communicate calmly and directly)

Does this person or relationship respond positively to your new behaviors, or do you lower yourself to their level? (Ex: Yes, they are more open to listening to my feelings and needs or no, they continue to dismiss my bids for connection and communication.)

We can't grow in environments that cause us to remain the same. Studies show that our surroundings greatly impact our ability to heal and evolve. When we stay in dynamics that reinforce old wounds or unhealthy patterns, our growth is stifled. Conversely, supportive relationships foster the safety and stability needed to challenge our insecurities and rewrite the narratives about ourselves and others. This is why it's essential to evaluate whether the people in your life support and mirror your efforts to create healthier relationship dynamics.

Reflect: How do my loved ones align with the healthy, secure relationships I strive for?

Understanding and Releasing Inherited Beliefs from Your Parents

Attachment studies reveal that relationship patterns stem from inherited beliefs. This visualization helps uncover your parents' influences and guides you to release them. You can listen to the guided visualization practice on my website at Jessica-DaSilvaCoaching.com/resources.

1. Sit or lie down, close your eyes, and take a few deep breaths.
2. Picture your caregivers as children (seeing a photo can help).
3. Imagine the home they grew up in. What do you notice? Is it warm and loving, or unstable and chaotic?
4. Visualize the key figures in their lives—parents, siblings, teachers, or others—who shaped their beliefs.
5. Ask yourself: What might they have been taught about love, safety, and self-worth?
6. Imagine your parents learning beliefs like "I'm unlovable. I'm a burden. I will be abandoned. I have to be perfect to be loved."
7. Now imagine these beliefs being packaged in a box and your caregivers giving it to you.
8. Visualize handing the box back to them with love, acknowledging their struggles and limitations without judgment. Say to yourself, "I release these beliefs with compassion and gratitude for what they taught me. I choose to create loving beliefs that support the life and relationship I desire."

Showing Compassion to Your Anxious Parts

Trying to "fix" our anxious attachment style often leads to shame, as these patterns are deeply embedded in our thoughts, feelings, and behaviors. Research shows that old attachment responses can resurface during distress, even after years of healing.

Parts work, as found in *Internal Family Systems Therapy* by Richard C. Schwartz and Martha Sweezy, teaches us that these less desirable aspects or parts of ourselves aren't bad but are protective mechanisms from our past. Instead of resisting or judging these parts, we learn to understand their role in our lives. My explanation differs from the core IFS framework, but it follows a similar concept. What are parts of your attachment style that you don't like?

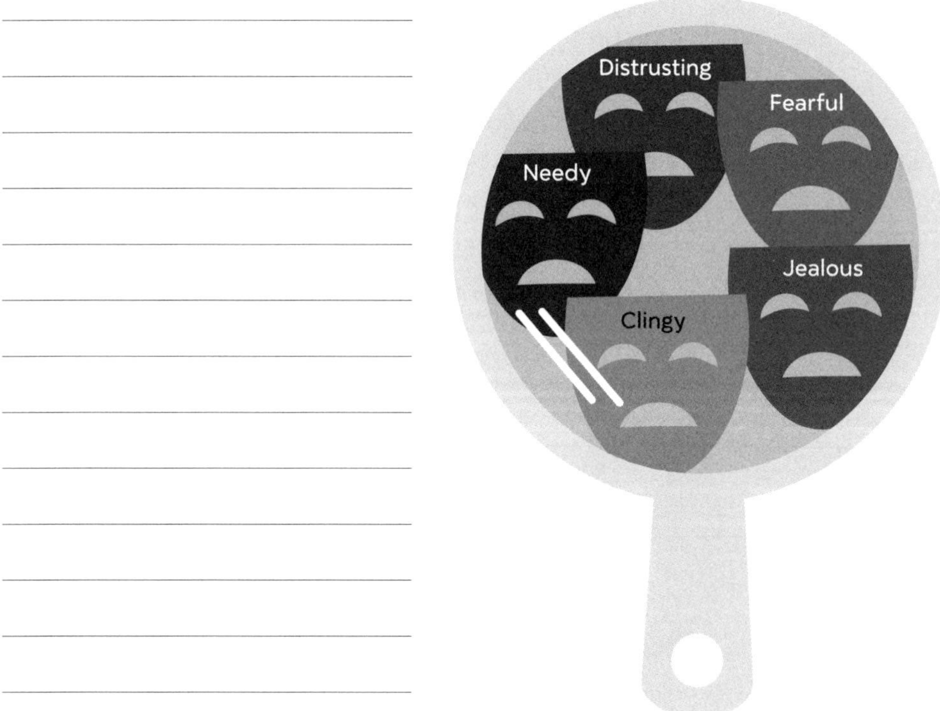

Give those parts names. (Ex: Needy Sally, Jealous Will, or Distrusting Jill)

What are these parts trying to protect you from? (Ex: Needy Sally is protecting me from feeling alone. Jealous Will is protecting me from being abandoned. Distrusting Jill is protecting me from being taken advantage of.)

CONTINUED >

CONTINUED FROM THE PREVIOUS PAGE

How have these parts helped you in the past? (Ex: Needy Sally has helped me get my needs met. Jealous Will has helped me address behaviors that were threatening to the relationship. Distrusting Jill has alerted me of red flags.)

Can you now begin to see these parts of yourself in a different light?

Your anxious parts were formed in your past to protect you from pain. They may have been the only effective way of keeping you safe and making sure your physical and emotional needs were met. However, as an adult, it's your responsibility to keep them in check and approach those insecure parts of you more compassionately and effectively. The goal is to use your parts to encourage thoughtful discernment instead of letting fear dominate your decisions and relationships.

In what ways are you grateful for your anxious parts? How have they helped protect or guide you in times of uncertainty or emotional challenges?

Re-Aligning with Your Relationship Values

By identifying and reconnecting to your values, you can develop a deeper connection to who you truly are and find and build relationships that align with your authentic self.

This checklist helps you clarify and prioritize your values in relationships.

IDENTIFY QUALITIES YOU ADMIRE IN HEALTHY RELATIONSHIPS

What qualities make for a strong and fulfilling relationship?
Examples:

- Togetherness
- Consistency
- Reliability
- Emotional Support
- Growth
- Mutual Respect
- Communication

____

____

____

____

____

____

____

____

____

DEFINE WHAT EACH VALUE LOOKS LIKE IN ACTION

How would these values be expressed in a relationship?
Examples:

- **Togetherness:** Makes an effort to spend time together and plan activities
- **Consistency:** Aligns words with actions
- **Growth:** Actively learns and improves ways to support the relationship without constant reminders
- **Emotional Support:** Listens and provides the support you need during challenging times

REFLECT ON YOUR PERSONAL PRIORITIES

Which of these values resonate most with me?

Are there additional values important to me that aren't listed?

RECOGNIZE PATTERNS IN PAST RELATIONSHIPS

Have I prioritized these values in my relationships?

What actions or behaviors aligned (or didn't align) with my values in the past?

VISUALIZE YOUR IDEAL RELATIONSHIP

What would a relationship look and feel like if it aligned with my values?

How can I use this understanding to build healthier, more fulfilling connections?

Transforming Your Relationship with Your Anxious Parts

This practice helps you connect with your anxious parts by approaching them with compassion, reducing their intensity, and creating a greater sense of stability.

1. Visualize your anxious parts:
   a. Get into a comfortable position and close your eyes.
   b. Imagine yourself in a place you feel relaxed, and invite aspects associated with your anxious attachment, such as a jealousy part, worried part, angry part, into that space. Notice that these parts may appear as a person, a feeling, or a symbol.
2. Connect with your anxious parts:
   a. Gently acknowledge that your parts are there. (Ex: I see that you're here because you're worried about me.)
      Begin a dialogue with your anxious parts. (Ex: "What are you afraid of right now?" or "What do you need from me to feel safer?")
   b. Offer reassurance as if you were speaking to a loved one who is in pain. (Ex: "I'm here for you" or "I got you.")
3. Integration:
   a. Imagine giving that part of you a hug and it gently fusing with you, becoming one. Feel into the comforting embrace.
4. Slowly come back into the present when you are ready.

To have the types of relationships we want, we must first familiarize ourselves with how that might feel and look. Remember that we unconsciously tend to repeat similar relationship dynamics from our past. However, with clarity around our values and the actions associated with someone who acts in alignment with those things that matter most to us, we can begin to recognize and appreciate those who have similar ways of experiencing love. A great way to do this is to become the person you want to be in relationship with.

Ask yourself: Who do I have to become to have the desired relationship I want?

Key Takeaways

Transforming your anxious attachment style is 100 percent possible. Bowlby indicated that by creating a secure "working model" for how we view ourselves, others, and relationships, we can experience the kinds of relationships we truly desire. Your past does not define your future, and by implementing new ways of thinking, feeling, and behaving, you can rewrite the narrative of your life.

Breaking your patterns, however, does take courage, patience, and compassion, as these ways of operating are deeply ingrained in your system. However, with consistent practice and a willingness to change, anyone can begin to cultivate secure attachment.

- By recognizing your anxious attachment patterns of thinking, feeling, and behaving, you can begin to shift them.
- Despite what your past has taught you, you can rewrite your present and future.
- Visualization is a powerful medium for connecting with your goals, aligning with your true desires, and helping you have what you truly want.
- Tools such as CBT, narrative therapy, parts work, and aligning with your values are effective strategies for breaking your insecure ways of experiencing yourself, others, and relationships.
- Consistency, patience, and compassion are key ingredients to helping you earn your secure attachment style.

"I am a powerful creator of my own life."

CHAPTER 4

OVERCOMING YOUR ANXIOUS ATTACHMENT

When we take the steps to align with a healthier, more secure version of ourselves, our self-esteem increases. When our self-esteem grows, we surround ourselves with people and experiences that match our internal state. We are more apt to notice people and relationships bringing us down and feel more empowered to set boundaries.

Aligning with our true selves in this way can be difficult, as we may disappoint people who are comfortable with easily accessing our resources and strengths. Honoring yourself and your feelings, needs, and boundaries may cause you to disrupt or even lose some relationships. But as I like to remind my students and clients, you have nothing to lose and everything to gain by being your most authentic self! People with an anxious attachment style have this underlying fear that if they show their true self or share their true feelings or desires, it will lead to abandonment and rejection. However, if that's the case, then you never had those people to begin with. By being your most authentic and vulnerable self, you quickly filter out the people who aren't positively contributing to your life and find those who are. It may take a little more time, but that's better than wasting your time.

Reclaiming Self-Empowerment Through Boundaries

Lisa was divorced from her husband of six years. However, they shared a house and had a child together. Leaning anxiously attached, Lisa had difficulty with her ex coming over as he pleased. Though living elsewhere, he was still contributing to the rent, and so Lisa felt obligated to allow him space for his things and access to the house. Though the financial support was helpful, the vague lines that defined their relationship brought about great distress. The unpredictable nature of their relationship caused her to remain attached to him. With this attachment came consistent hypervigilance, worry, uncertainty, sadness, and disappointment. Though their relationship had ended, she found herself submitting to his physical and emotional needs and becoming resentful in the process.

After many long sessions, by breaking through her fears of abandonment and guilt, she was able to set her limitations around their relationship, including removing his belongings and setting visiting hours to spend time with their child. Though her ex resisted her boundaries initially, she remained firm and even stated consequences, such as creating a custody agreement if he was not cooperative. Not only was she able to finally emotionally detach from her ex, but she gained a newfound sense of confidence and self-empowerment by honoring herself.

"Daring to set boundaries is about having the courage to love ourselves, even when we risk disappointing others."

—BRENÉ BROWN

Connecting to Your Self-Worth

We are born as blank slates, and our experiences shape our beliefs, including self-worth. The good news: We can rewire our minds by identifying, challenging, and replacing limiting beliefs with ones that build confidence. This exercise will help you begin that transformative process.

What were moments in my childhood when I felt unimportant, unseen, or less-than? (Ex: When my mom told me she didn't have time for me, or when my dad chose work over spending time with me.)

How did these moments shape the way I viewed myself? (Ex: I saw myself as not being important or deserving of love.)

CONTINUED >

CONTINUED FROM THE PREVIOUS PAGE

How did this perception of myself impact my choices in relationships? (Ex: I felt as though I had to earn love, overcompensate, and choose partners that prioritized their needs.)

Considering I now know where I learned these beliefs, are they true about me, or is it an insecurity? (Ex: It's an insecurity.)

What do I want to believe about myself instead? (Ex: I am worthy of having a mutually supportive relationship.)

What steps can I take to align with my self-worth? (Ex: I can repeat positive affirmations, respect my boundaries, and practice self-compassion.)

Affirmations are an excellent way to create new belief systems that align with how you desire to view and experience yourself. Repeat these affirmations to yourself daily. Put reminders on your phone or notes around your space.

What are the beliefs that someone with self-worth has?

Example:

I am worthy of healthy love.
I love and accept myself for exactly who I am.
I deserve to be happy.
I deserve to feel cherished.
I deserve to get my needs met.
I deserve respect.

Tip: If these feel hard for you to say, use "I am learning to believe..." to bridge the gap.

Do You Struggle with Setting Boundaries?

Boundaries are limits we set to protect our well-being. People with an anxious attachment style often prioritize external validation over their own needs, fearing rejection if they say "no" or enforce boundaries. This pattern can lead to diminished self-worth, resentment, and unhappiness.

Think about the key relationships in your life (e.g., partner, friends, family, coworkers). Answer the following questions with "yes" or "no":

Do you often feel drained after interacting with certain people?

Yes / No

Do you say yes to things you don't want to do to avoid conflict or disappointment?

Yes / No

CONTINUED >

CONTINUED FROM THE PREVIOUS PAGE

Do you feel responsible for other people's emotions or problems and feel the need to fix them?
Yes / No

Do you feel guilty or selfish when you take time for yourself?
Yes / No

Do you hesitate to express your opinions, especially when they differ from others?
Yes / No

Do you say things you don't mean just to keep the peace?
Yes / No

Do you often break promises you make to yourself?
Yes / No

Are you overly critical of yourself or let your inner critic dominate your thoughts?
Yes / No

RESULTS

If you answered **"yes"** to most of these questions, you likely struggle with setting boundaries. Recognizing this is the first step toward creating healthier, more balanced relationships.

Visualize Your Worthy Self

Visualization is a shortcut to becoming the version of yourself you aspire to be by creating new neural pathways. When you vividly imagine a scenario—in this case, your worthy self—it activates the same regions in your brain as if you were actually experiencing it. By doing this practice consistently, you will create new connections in the brain aligned with more positive and empowering outcomes.

Upon waking up or going to sleep, take 5 minutes to close your eyes and visualize yourself as being worthy.

- Think about what you are wearing, your posture, your demeanor, and the way you present yourself to the world.
- Think about the types of relationships you have. Are they rooted in mutual respect and support? Do you feel loved, cherished, and cared for?
- Think about how you approach challenging situations with your self-awareness and confidence.
- Think about how you communicate your feelings and needs.
- Think about how you stick up for yourself and set boundaries.
- Most importantly, allow yourself to feel the emotions that arise as you think about your worthy self.
- Take action as this version of you!

Tip: If you struggle with this exercise, think about someone you view as having self-worth and put yourself in their shoes.

How may I look at boundaries as being an act of self-love rather than being selfish?

Complete the following prompts:

When I set a boundary, I show myself love by... (Ex: honoring my need for self-care, even if it means saying no to someone.)

Boundaries allow me to care for myself because... (Ex: they create space for me to recharge and show up fully for others later.)

I can give love to others more freely when I have boundaries because... (Ex: I'm not operating from a place of resentment or exhaustion.)

Communicating Boundaries

Communicating boundaries means identifying your feelings and needs while setting clear consequences to ensure others understand and respect your limitations.

Use the chart below to identify a situation where you may need to set boundaries.

STEP	QUESTION	EXAMPLE RESPONSE
Identify the Situation	What is a situation you won't tolerate anymore?	When my partner yells at me when stressed.
Identify Your Feelings	How does this situation make you feel?	It makes me feel disrespected.
Understand Why	Why does this make you feel this way?	Because it's an aggressive and hurtful tone.
Determine Your Need	What do you need to feel better about this situation?	I need to be spoken to calmly in moments of stress.
Set a Consequence	What actionable step will you take if this boundary is not respected?	I will leave the room when he raises his voice.

Practice setting boundaries in this format:
I feel __________ because of __________. I need __________, or else __________.

BOUNDARY STATEMENT EXAMPLE

"I feel afraid when you yell at me during moments of high stress. I need you to speak to me calmly, or else I will leave the room."
Boundaries are there to protect you, not control others. By communicating them clearly, you can better understand how others respect your needs.

Notice what fears arise when you consider setting a boundary. For those with anxious attachment, these fears often stem from a deep worry about rejection or abandonment, leading us to suppress our true selves to preserve the connection and peace we crave. By identifying and acknowledging these fears, you can begin to challenge them.

Ask yourself:

What is the absolute worst-case scenario if I set this boundary? Can I be certain this will happen? If it does, how will I handle it?

Reflecting on these questions helps you build resilience, trust in yourself, and confidence to set boundaries without fear dictating your actions.

Observing Your Boundaries on a Day-to-Day Basis

There are three different types of boundaries. Loose boundaries are seen when we mostly neglect our feelings and needs. Rigid boundaries, on the other hand, are when we mostly think about our own feelings and needs. Loose and rigid boundaries live on opposite sides of the scale and anxious attachments can exhibit both, depending on the circumstances. The goal is to create flexible boundaries, where you allow yourself to give when it feels right, say no when necessary, and adapt thoughtfully without compromising your self-respect or well-being.

As you go about your daily life, notice your interactions with others and when you engage in loose, rigid, or flexible boundaries.

- **Loose boundary example:** Despite feeling frustrated and overwhelmed, you say "yes" every time because you don't want to disappoint others or risk conflict.
- **Rigid boundary example:** You refuse to share personal feelings, concerns, or vulnerabilities with others, believing it will protect you from getting hurt.
- **Flexible boundary example:** You acknowledge that you feel emotionally or mentally drained at this time and communicate your limits respectfully.

With practice and self-awareness, you can move toward creating boundaries that nurture healthier relationships and a greater sense of personal well-being.

Navigating the Guilt

Research shows that guilt often follows setting boundaries, as we fear disappointing others or facing negative consequences like being called selfish or losing affection. These beliefs stem from past experiences and lead us to appease others despite discomfort. Just as we form beliefs about relationships, we also form beliefs about emotions. This exercise will help you reframe guilt and break free from its hold.

What am I feeling guilty for? (Ex: saying no to a girl's trip with my friends)

Where do I feel the guilt in my body? (Ex: in my chest)

Can I sit with this guilt momentarily and hold space for it without fixing it? (Ex: yes)

Is it true that I should feel guilty about setting this boundary? (Ex: No, I have every right to say no even if my friends don't agree.)

How would I view this situation if I could remove the guilt from my experience? (Ex: I would more freely set boundaries without feeling bad.)

Practice reminding yourself that your perception of guilt can either hinder you or motivate you to set boundaries. Reframe the way you view boundaries. (Ex: I choose to see boundaries as helpful in my life.)

Remember that your feelings guide you to your needs. When you feel good around people, your body indicates that your needs for security and safety are being met. Likewise, when you feel bad around people, your body indicates that your needs for security and safety are going unmet.

Who in your life makes you feel bad or guilty for setting boundaries?

Do you feel mostly emotionally safe or unsafe around this person?

Do you find that keeping this person in your life is hurting or helping you?

Consider if this person were no longer in your life. Do you feel relief, freedom, peace?

Forgiving Yourself and Others

Honoring yourself often involves moments of disappointing others, but it's an act of self-love. Reflecting on how certain people or situations have affected you may bring up anger, guilt, or resentment. To move forward with clarity and balance, it's important to release these emotional burdens.

The Hawaiian practice of *Ho'oponopono* is a simple yet powerful tool for letting go and finding peace.

1. Sit comfortably, take deep breaths, and center yourself.
2. Find a quiet place: Reflect on a specific person, situation, or feeling causing emotional weight.
3. Recite the Ho'oponopono Mantra:
   a. *"I'm Sorry"*: Acknowledge responsibility for your role in the situation
   b. *"Please Forgive Me"*: Release guilt and surrender to peace
   c. *"Thank You"*: Appreciate the lessons learned, even in difficult experiences
   d. *"I Love You"*: Send love to yourself and others, fostering compassion
4. Reflect and release: Let emotions flow without judgment.

Practice this mantra regularly to lighten your emotional load, cultivate inner peace, and deepen your self-love. You don't necessarily have to forgive others if you're not ready or willing, but this practice can help you release the emotional grip they have on you, shift your focus inward, and find peace within yourself.

So What if They Leave?

When setting boundaries, we must be prepared for all possible outcomes. This uncertainty can be extremely unsettling for many people, but it is the most empowering action step you can take for yourself to cultivate self-love, self-trust, and self-worth.

We want to make sure we're asserting our boundaries from the very beginning of our relationship so that we can more easily assess compatibility and show people from the get-go what we need to feel safe. However, if you begin to set boundaries years into your relationship, others may not be as flexible to your requests. Regardless, set your boundaries. It's never too late to begin honoring yourself. Your health, well-being, and happiness are on the line!

Do you notice that you have guilt, resentment, or anger toward yourself or others?

____

____

How is holding on to this guilt, resentment, or anger hurting or hindering you?

____

____

What would life feel like if this guilt, resentment, or anger no longer existed in your life?

____

____

How would you approach life differently if free of these emotions and ties?

Set a timer for 3 to 5 minutes and practice visualizing yourself free from guilt, resentment, or anger. Notice the freedom, peace, and liberation that comes with letting go of these emotions and how you approach life in a new way.

"I am not responsible for how people respond to my boundaries. I am responsible for setting and honoring my boundaries. If my relationships end because I set boundaries, it's a sign that the foundation was cracked. In healthy relationships, I can set boundaries without fears of retaliation, cut-offs, or manipulation."

—NEDRA GLOVER TAWWAB

Key Takeaways

Making ourselves a priority is essential for maintaining our mental health and well-being. When we consider our feelings and needs and take steps to honor ourselves in these ways, we increase our sense of self-worth. The more we take action in these self-loving ways, the more confident and self-assured we become. Rather than people-pleasing and adhering to the desires of others, when we are honest about who we are and what we want, we get to see people's true colors and can begin to assess who is here to support us. Remember that you have nothing to lose and everything to gain by being your most authentic self. Remember that you have nothing to lose and everything to gain by being your most authentic self.

- Just because you have low self-worth now doesn't mean it can't increase. Honoring your feelings and needs and taking care of yourself can make you feel more deserving and valuable.
- Boundaries are not selfish. They are essential for self-care and teaching people how we want to be treated.
- When learning to say no and setting our limitations, guilt is a common emotion we may experience. Acknowledge and release it.
- Forgive yourself and others in order to move forward in your life with more clarity and freedom.

CHAPTER 5

MINDFULNESS AND SELF-REGULATION

It's inspiring to see clinicians and individuals embracing a more holistic approach to trauma-informed care and healing practices. Just as it's important to understand our mind and the beliefs that influence our behavioral patterns, it's crucial to focus on the body and ways in which to regulate our nervous system, as both are deeply interconnected.

By incorporating practices such as mindfulness, compassion, attuning to one's feelings and needs in a balanced way, and implementing emotional regulation exercises daily, we will not only feel more stable and secure within ourselves, we can more confidently and authentically understand and support those we love. When approaching our triggers and insecurities from a dysregulated space, such as coping in the fight, flight, freeze, or fawn response, we often behave in ways that are harmful to ourselves and others, despite our justifications in the moment.

Meeting our needs in these more reactive ways may have worked when we were younger, but it is no longer productive as adults. When we learn to regulate our nervous system, we can approach challenging emotions and situations with clarity and proactivity. This newfound way of experiencing yourself creates the building blocks for cultivating secure, authentic connections.

From Reactive Behaviors to Intentional Growth

Antonio was a highly anxious person in his relationships. He craved attention, understanding, and a profound sense of connection in his romantic relationships, but he always found himself with people who were incapable of or unwilling to meet his needs. When his needs were unmet, he would become highly activated and resort to unhelpful protest behaviors such as blaming or criticizing, passive-aggressiveness, and the silent treatment in hopes that his partners would begin to take him seriously. Unsurprisingly, his partners, often leaning more avoidant, would deactivate by becoming defensive and avoiding communication. These reactions left Antonio feeling more alone, deprived, and "needy." Hungry for reconnection and reassurance that his relationship was still intact, he would apologize for his behaviors and try to make amends by denying his feelings and needs and prioritizing the comfort of those he loved. Logically, he couldn't sustain neglecting himself for very long—he would soon become triggered and resort to the same old ways of seeking the attention and love he deeply craved.

By learning to understand his triggers, regulate his emotions in times of distress, and meet his underlying needs in healthier ways, Antonio could approach his challenges confidently and create connections that aligned with his true values and desires.

"Attachment principles teach us that most people are only as needy as their unmet needs."

—AMIR LEVINE AND RACHEL HELLER

Showing Yourself Mindful Self-Compassion

People who have an anxious attachment style can feel very alone in their pain and emotional deprivation. This isolation can deepen their shame and beliefs about being unlovable and insignificant. Mindful Self-Compassion is a beautiful therapeutic approach developed by Christopher Germer and Kristin Neff to help people approach their inner challenges with mindfulness, kindness, and common humanity.

Use this table to practice mindful self-compassion by reflecting on your emotions, showing kindness to yourself, and connecting to common humanity.

COMPONENT	ACTION	EXAMPLE REFLECTION
Mindfulness	Observe your emotional experience without labeling it as "good" or "bad."	*"I feel alone right now and as though nobody loves me."*
Self-Kindness	Show yourself grace and compassion instead of judging or criticizing yourself.	*"It's okay to feel this way. These emotions don't mean anything negative about my worth."*
Common Humanity	Remind yourself that pain is a part of the shared human experience and you are not alone.	*"Everyone experiences loneliness at times. I know there are people who will care and support me."*

HOW TO USE THE TABLE

1. Identify an emotional challenge you're currently facing.
2. Work through each component by reflecting and completing the corresponding action.
3. Write your thoughts in the "Example Reflection" column for personal insight.

CONTINUED >

CONTINUED FROM THE PREVIOUS PAGE

COMPONENT	ACTION	EXAMPLE REFLECTION
Mindfulness	Observe your emotional experience without labeling it as "good" or "bad."	
Self-Kindness	Show yourself grace and compassion instead of judging or criticizing yourself.	
Common Humanity	Remind yourself that pain is a part of the shared human experience and you are not alone.	

When you are in distress, how do you tend to talk to yourself? For instance, do you call yourself names or become highly self-critical? Do you compare yourself to others and feel ashamed that other people have it better than you? Do you inflict self-harm?

Begin to notice these automatic reactions and instead choose to show yourself compassion. For example, think about how you would ideally be treated in moments of pain. What are the words you want to hear, the tone of voice that would feel soothing, and the actions that reassure you that you are loved and safe? Practice approaching yourself in this way.

Are You Emotionally Dysregulated in Your Relationships?

Use this questionnaire to help you assess how you may be experiencing emotional dysregulation in your relationship.

Do you often feel tension or tightness in your body or changes in your breathing patterns? **Yes / No**

Do you feel a persistent sense of restlessness or inability to concentrate on things outside of your relationship? **Yes / No**

Do you often feel overwhelmed, anxious, or irritable without a clear reason? **Yes / No**

Do you experience mood swings or difficulty regulating your emotions? **Yes / No**

Are you constantly scanning for signs of rejection, disinterest, or emotional unavailability? **Yes / No**

Do you struggle with impulsivity, overreacting, or difficulty calming yourself in distress? **Yes / No**

Do you become highly needy or clingy in your relationships when triggered? **Yes / No**

 **SCORING AND REFLECTION:**

Count your "Yes" answers.

0–2 Yes Responses: Your nervous system is likely operating in a mostly balanced state, with occasional dysregulation.

3–6 Yes Responses: You may be showing moderate signs of nervous system dysregulation and might benefit from practicing self-regulation techniques and getting support.

7 Yes Responses: Your nervous system shows significant signs of dysregulation. Seeking professional guidance can help you address your distress.

Box Breathing

As cliché as it sounds, learning to breathe effectively is crucial for regulating your emotions and feeling more stable in your body. Certain types of breathing can activate the parasympathetic nervous system, which is responsible for calming and relaxing your body. When we are able to bring our bodies into this more peaceful state, we can make better informed decisions for our lives rather than acting impulsively on our more uncomfortable emotions.

Box breathing has been popularized by Mark Divine, a retired Navy SEAL Commander. It is a simple yet effective technique to manage stress and gain emotional control. The technique involves controlling your breath in four equal parts, creating a "boxlike" rhythm.

---

1. Inhale through your nose for 4 counts.
2. Hold your breath for 4 counts.
3. Exhale through your mouth for 4 counts.
4. Hold your breath again for 4 counts.
5. Repeat this breathing exercise 4 more times or as needed.

This practice can help you feel more grounded, clearheaded, and in control, no matter the situation. With consistency, regulating yourself will feel habitual. Over time, it can become a powerful tool to support emotional resilience and self-regulation.

Our relationships can greatly influence the state of our nervous system. By assessing how we feel in our relationships on a day-to-day basis, we can better assess if our relationships are negatively or positively impacting our lives.

- Do you fear abandonment or rejection?
- Do you walk on eggshells to avoid conflict?
- Are you constantly hypervigilant?
- Do you suppress your feelings to appease your partner?
- Do you overthink?
- Do emotions feel overwhelming or controlling?
- Do you struggle to relax in your relationship?

Take note of how frequently these feelings arise to better understand their effect on your well-being.

Three Steps to Identifying Your Relationship Needs

One of the most important things we can do for ourselves is to learn to recognize our relationship needs. The way we think, feel, and behave stems from our primal need to satisfy certain core requirements for survival, well-being, and fulfillment. Just as humans have physiological needs for air, food, shelter, and water, we also have psychological needs for connection, belonging, affection, autonomy, and validation, for example. When we can identify our needs, we can be proactive in meeting them. A simple way to determine our needs is through first attuning to our feelings. For example, feelings of loneliness may indicate a need for connection, while frustration might point to unmet needs for respect or understanding. By identifying our needs, we can be proactive in meeting them moving forward.

Three Steps to Identifying Your Needs:

What am I feeling?
(Ex: I feel afraid)

____

____

Why am I feeling this way?
(Ex: My partner and I got into a heated argument)

____

____

What do I need to feel better?
(Ex: I need reassurance that they still love me)

____

____

Our relationship needs are often tied to the things we lacked in our earliest relationship dynamics. For those of us with an anxious attachment style, that may look like a need for attunement, attention, belonging, consistency, and predictability.

How did your caregivers often make you feel when you needed them?

What did they do to make you feel this way?

What did you need from them to feel safe and secure?

These reflections can help you identify and understand your underlying relationship needs as an adult. This understanding can pave the way for positive change and a more fulfilling future.

Emotional Freedom Technique (EFT) for Transforming Painful Emotions

EFT is a wonderful emotion regulation tool. This practice helps you acknowledge your challenges and the emotional experiences tied to them, and then let them go through tapping on specific acupressure points. The process combines physical tapping as you talk about the difficult emotional experience, which helps calm the nervous system, release emotional tension, and reframe the way you look at your circumstances. By focusing on both emotional and physical sensation, EFT can help you self-soothe and restore emotional balance. You can find a guided EFT practice on my website at JessicaDaSilvaCoaching.com/resources.

1. Select the problem you'd like to address. (Ex: I want to address my anger.)
2. Assess your level of pain from 1–5.
3. Create your setup statement: "Even though I feel ____________, I deeply love and accept myself."
4. Perform the tapping sequence on the EFT points as shown on the diagram by using 2 or 3 fingers to gently tap 5 or 7 times per point, while repeating the set-up statement. Feel free to talk through what you're experiencing while making sure to end with positive feelings, such as "Even though I feel __________, I know this emotion will pass and that I am here for myself."
5. Reassess your pain level and perform more tapping rounds if needed.

CONTINUED >

CONTINUED FROM THE PREVIOUS PAGE

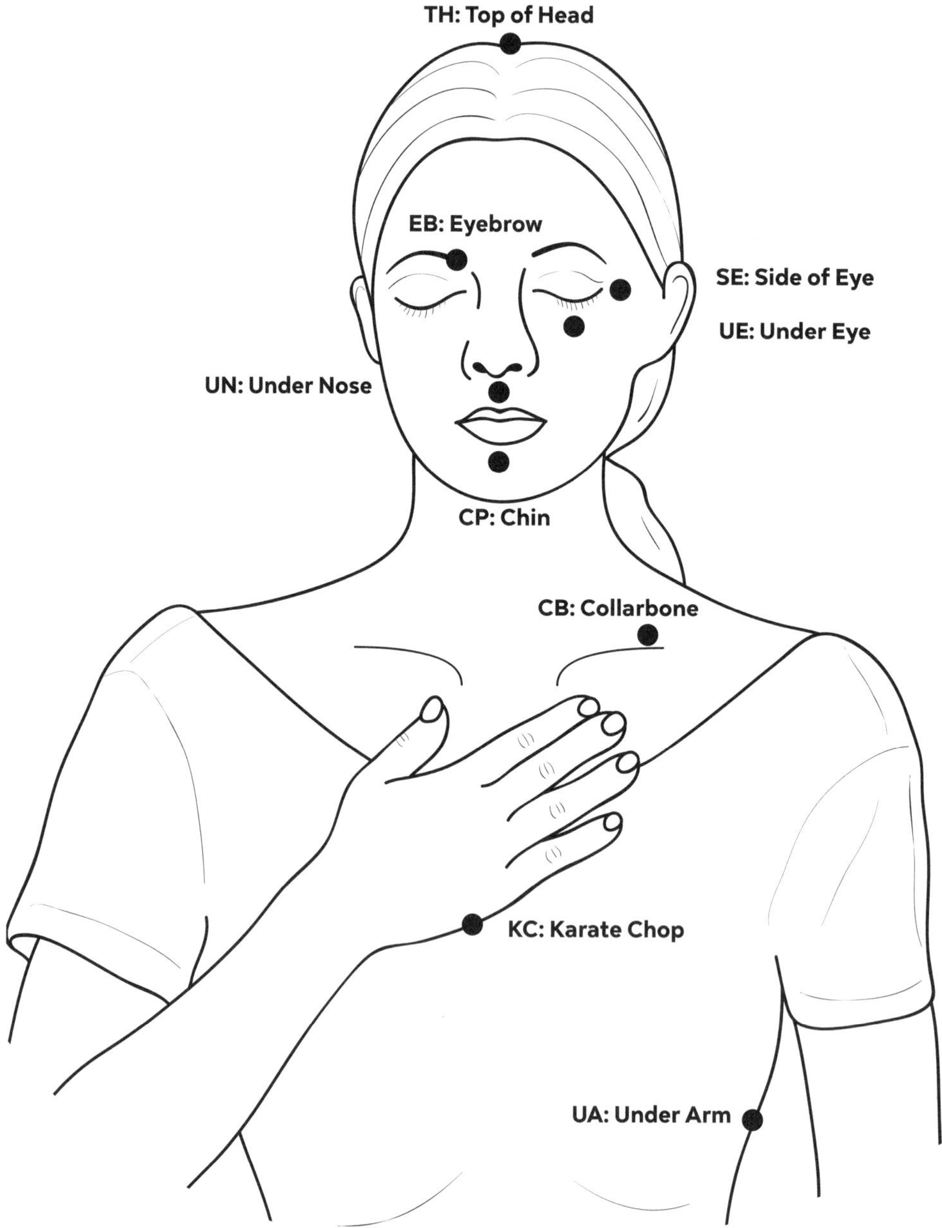

EFT Tapping Points

How to Communicate Your Needs in a Healthy Way

Communication, communication, communication. We hear this term everywhere in the therapeutic realm, and for good reason! Many of us were not taught healthy ways of communicating. If you have an anxious attachment style, you might communicate your feelings and needs indirectly using behaviors like making passive-aggressive remarks, giving the silent treatment, expressing anger through outbursts, dropping subtle hints, showing frustrated body language, or sharing stories about others in the hope that your partner will read between the lines and understand what you deeply want or need.

Don't shame yourself for how you used to communicate—it was a survival response to unmet needs and a lack of healthy examples. As adults, however, we are responsible for learning proactive ways of communicating to cultivate healthier relationships.

A helpful format for proactively communicating your needs is seen in Marshall B. Rosenberg's book *Nonviolent Communication*:

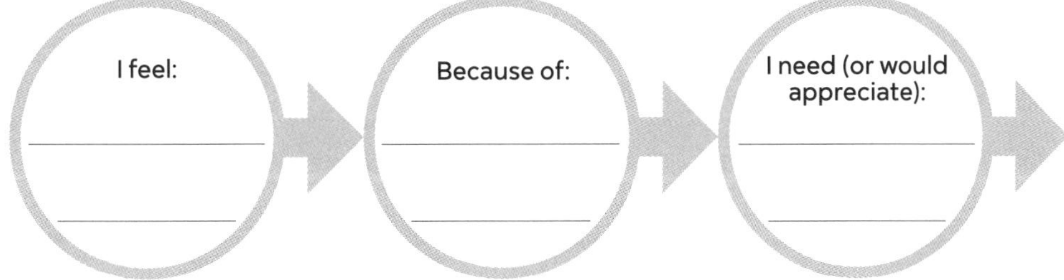

Consider where your needs might not currently be met, and use this format to formulate an "I feel" response.

Ex: I feel unimportant because you spend weekends with your friends instead of me. I'd appreciate planning a day for quality time together.

After writing your statement in the diagram box, practice saying it out loud, first to yourself and then to others.

CONTINUED >

CONTINUED FROM THE PREVIOUS PAGE

Have you noticed that when triggered, you will impulsively say or do something hurtful that works against your desired outcome? For example, you might lash out when you want reassurance or withdraw when you crave connection. These reactive behaviors often stem from unprocessed emotions and unmet needs, making it harder to resolve situations in a healthy way.

Reflect on your day and record any moments when you felt triggered or distressed, along with the impulsive reactions you wanted to act on. Moving forward, use this awareness to pause, breathe, and consider how you can directly communicate your feelings and needs instead.

Meeting Your Needs in Healthy Ways

Learning to meet our needs in a balanced way is crucial for relationship harmony. People with an anxious attachment style often believe that their partner should meet all or most of their needs, or that they should have similar needs to them. However, these are unrealistic expectations often rooted in codependency and enmeshment. Humans have differing needs, and assuming that other people experience love the way we do is a recipe for disappointment.

Instead, aim to become an interdependent human, where you learn to balance meeting your needs on your own with meeting your needs through your loved ones. This involves recognizing that no person can fulfill all your emotional needs and that healthy relationships are built on a balance of give and take. By becoming aware of your needs and making small efforts to fulfill those needs, you will foster a sense of individuality, self-confidence, self-trust, and relationship harmony.

In the circles on the following page, list different ways that you can meet your needs. This will begin to satiate your desires for care, connection, and fulfillment, helping you feel more grounded and self-sufficient while reducing the need to seek validation or fulfillment solely from one person.

CONTINUED >

CONTINUED FROM THE PREVIOUS PAGE

COMMUNITY
Ex: Groups, classes, activities, volunteering, projects...

PEOPLE
Ex: Friends, family, colleagues, therapist, coaches, mentors...

RESOURCES
Ex: Podcasts, books, social media pages, music, YouTube...

SELF-CARE PRACTICES
Ex: Meditation, affirmations, journaling, breathing, EFT, emotional regulation...

Assessing How Others React to Your Healthy Expression of Needs

This practice will help you assess whether the people in your life are acknowledging and responding to your efforts in communicating your feelings and needs in a healthier way. Through these observations, you can see whether they are contributing to or hindering your journey toward secure relationships.

Reflect on the specific ways you are expressing your feelings and needs in a healthier way. (Ex: When I am upset, rather than becoming passive, I express what I'm feeling and needing in the "feel __ and I need ___" form.)

Over the next month, observe how the people in your life respond to your changes:

- Do they listen when I approach them calmly and directly?
- Do they value my efforts?
- Are they responsive to meeting my concerns, or do they dismiss me?

Reflect on your observations. (Ex: Do I feel emotionally supported and valued in this relationship? Are they responsive to my communication, or do they resist it?)

Express gratitude for their effort if they're supportive and seek help to address challenges if they're willing. However, if the relationship consistently hinders your growth, consider whether it's worth continuing.

To determine whether to meet a need yourself or through your partner, consider answering the following questions:

What is the specific need I'm trying to meet? (Ex: reassurance, validation, quality time, or comfort)

____

____

____

____

Can this need be reasonably met by me? Am I looking for external validation for something I can affirm in myself?

Is this need reasonable to ask of my partner? Does meeting this need involve collaboration or compromise that strengthens our relationship?

Will involving my partner enhance our relationship or create unnecessary strain? Is this a moment for collaboration or a chance for me to grow independently?

"I am more than capable of meeting my own needs. Meeting my own needs builds self-confidence and trust."

Key Takeaways

By reading this chapter, you now have a better understanding of how mindfulness, self-compassion, emotional regulation tools, and honoring your needs can help you feel more stable and confident in yourself and your relationships. Developing a secure attachment style requires more than just being aware of your challenges. You must also implement skills needed to think, feel, and behave in ways that are more aligned with your desires and goals.

We can't change by remaining the same. To break our anxious attachment patterns, we must step out of our comfort zones, challenge old habits, and create new secure patterns for connection. As with learning anything new, please be patient with yourself.

- Mindful self-compassion can help you observe your pain without judgment. Instead, you can show kindness to yourself and remember that you are not alone in your suffering.
- Practicing emotional regulation tools such as box breathing and EFT can shift your anxiety into feelings of calm and clarity.
- You can make healthier, proactive decisions with an emotionally regulated nervous system.
- Understanding your feelings and needs and learning to meet them in healthy, balanced ways is crucial for harmonious relationships. This insight also clarifies relationship compatibility and support.

PART III

DEVELOPING LASTING RELATIONSHIPS

The tools in this workbook were created to help you navigate your anxious attachment challenges by building healthier habits for relating to yourself and others. In part three, you will be guided through exercises, strategies, practices, and affirmations aimed at helping you sustain a healthy and secure attachment style in your relationships.

One of the biggest concerns I hear from clients after our time working together has ended is "What if I mess this up?" However, by practicing these tools on a continuous basis and making them a part of your lifestyle rather than a temporary commitment, you will slowly but surely create unshakable habits that will empower you to continue growing and becoming the most secure version of yourself.

This section will encourage you to use the tools in this workbook to not only find the relationships you want but also maintain the ones you have. Most importantly, I want to remind you that your relationship with yourself is the most vital of them all, as we can't give from an empty cup. Creating a secure attachment style means learning to prioritize yourself, first and foremost, so that you can give and receive love in healthy and balanced ways.

CHAPTER 6

DEVELOPING SECURE ATTACHMENTS

Do you have a pattern of rescuing those around you? Perhaps you've built an identity around your over-functioning and over-giving nature. Maybe you find yourself in relationships with emotionally unavailable people who seem to take more than they give. Yet you still stay, hoping that they will one day show up for you in the way you deeply desire—but that day never seems to come.

If this sounds like you, then you may be codependent. Codependency is prevalent in people who have an anxious attachment style. Although dependency is natural and healthy within balanced relationships, codependency is unhealthy, as we rely solely on our attachment figures for our sense of self-worth, belonging, and emotional stability. In codependency, we over-function, struggle to set boundaries, and feel an overwhelming responsibility to save others from their pain. This dynamic can leave us feeling unappreciated, exhausted, and resentful, as our needs often go unmet while we prioritize the well-being of others.

This chapter will guide you in recognizing how codependency may be affecting your life. It will provide you with exercises and practices that, when actively engaged with, can help you break out of these unfulfilling roles and into a place of wholeness.

The Girl Who Can Do It All: Why Over-Giving in Relationships Isn't Sustainable

Jessica appeared to be a strong, independent woman in her community, ambitious and always striving to improve her life. She took pride in the love, attention, and support she offered in her relationships but often found her efforts weren't reciprocated. Early in her relationships, Jessica presented herself as easygoing, self-sufficient, and needless, in an attempt to increase her appeal to the partners she was attracted to. However, as the relationships progressed, she lost sight of herself, spiraling into anxiety and depression.

In addition to presenting herself as cool and self-sufficient, she would later become hyper-focused on meeting her partner's needs and desires, breaking her back to make them happy, even at the expense of her personal well-being. From her attachment perspective, if the ones she loved were comfortable and happy, that validated her sense of self and worth within her relationships and in life. However, this way of operating was not sustainable, as she found herself resentful, depressed, and unsupported in the process.

By recognizing her codependent tendencies and focusing on becoming whole within herself, Jessica cultivated a stronger sense of self-worth, free from the constant need for external validation.

That Jessica is me.

"Don't set yourself on fire trying to keep others warm."

—PENNY REID

Are You Codependent?

This exercise helps you identify if you struggle with codependency by examining patterns of prioritizing others' needs over your own, leading to feelings of burnout.

Do you feel responsible for making your loved ones happy?
Yes / No
Are you often over-functioning in your relationships, doing for others what they can do for themselves?
Yes / No

Do you feel your worth is tied to how much others need or depend on you?
Yes / No

Do you try to save or rescue others from their pain and suffering?
Yes / No

Do you pride yourself on how much you give or sacrifice for others?
Yes / No

Do you often put your needs or desires on the back burner in relationships?
Yes / No

Do you become angry or resentful when your loved ones don't give to you in similar ways?
Yes / No

Do you feel bad saying no or guilty when you set boundaries with your loved ones?
Yes / No

Do you believe that if you don't help your loved one, they'll fail or won't cope without you?
Yes / No

You may be codependent if you answered "Yes" to three or more of these questions.

Reflect on how your self-sacrificing behaviors in relationships, while draining to your mental and physical health, may temporarily fulfill certain emotional needs. What are the underlying needs driving these codependent tendencies? Consider how shifting from external validation to internal self-worth might impact your sense of self and the quality of your connections. Reflect on what steps you can take to prioritize your needs without compromising your authenticity.

The Root of Your Need to Earn Love

People with an anxious attachment style are notorious for pairing with avoidantly attached individuals because their relationship role mirrors similar childhood experiences, where love and attention may have felt conditional or unreliable. This perpetuates a cycle of trying to earn affection or closeness.

Answer the questions below to identify your patterns for earning love:

How did I have to earn love in my childhood? (Ex: Doing all the chores and being my mom's emotional crutch)

How do I have to earn love in my current relationships? (Ex: Breaking the bank to support all my partner's dreams)

Where did I feel as though love was conditional in my childhood? (Ex: To get acknowledgment, I had to get good grades and do what I was told.)

Where do I feel as though love is conditional in my current relationships? (Ex: I feel I have to cook, clean, and take care of kids to get acknowledgment from my partner.)

Where did I feel as though I had to chase connection in my childhood? (Ex: Listening to my dad complain just to spend time with him)

Where do I feel as though I have to chase connection in my current relationships? (Ex: Agreeing to plans I'm not excited about just to spend time with my partner)

Future Pacing with Your Codependency

Future pacing is a powerful tool that allows us to see the potential consequences of our codependent behaviors. When we're immersed in our current circumstances, it's difficult to recognize the impact of our actions. However, by projecting ourselves into the future and imagining the outcomes of our current behaviors, we can gain a clearer perspective. This exercise helps us see if the life we're living is truly the one we want for ourselves.

1. Find a comfortable position and take a moment to relax.
2. Close your eyes and breathe deeply, allowing your body to unwind.
3. Imagine that you are looking into a mirror and seeing your reflection one year from now as if you were still operating in your codependent and over-functioning ways. How do you look? How do you feel? Are you happy?
4. Now fast-forward five years, and you are still operating in the same patterns. How do you look? How do you feel? Are you happy?
5. Now fast-forward ten years, and you are still operating in the same patterns. How do you look? How do you feel? Are you happy?

Note the consequences of remaining the same on your mental and physical health and well-being. Earning love was perhaps your only way of receiving the kind of care, love, and attention you needed in your earlier relationship dynamics. However, as an adult, you now recognize that these ways of operating are unhealthy.

On the following page, identify the short-term benefits you gain from earning love and the long-term repercussions. By recognizing how these behaviors serve you in the moment but hinder you over time, you can start making choices that align with your long-term emotional health.

What are the short-term benefits of earning love? (Ex: Gaining temporary connection)

What are the long-term repercussions of earning love? (Ex: Neglecting my own needs and authenticity)

Compromising vs. Self-Neglecting

Every human is equipped with unique needs, desires, perspectives, and ways of experiencing life and relationships. To coexist with others, we must be mindful of our differences and find ways to compromise or meet in the middle.

While compromise is a mutual collaboration where both people's needs and desires are considered, self-neglecting is when we ignore or deprioritize our needs or desires to cater to others.

To create more balance in our relationships, we need to recognize when we are prioritizing others' needs and desires at the expense of our own and learn to assert ourselves to ensure our needs are also valued and met.

Using the common examples below, evaluate whether you are leaning more toward healthy compromise or falling into patterns of self-neglect.

Where are your currently compromising "meeting in the middle" in relationships?

Examples:
- Financial decisions.
- How we spend time with family.
- Preparing meals.

Where are you currently self-neglecting "prioritizing yourself" in relationships?

Examples:
- Doing all of the house chores.
- Prioritizing their goals.
- Taking on all of the emotional responsibility.

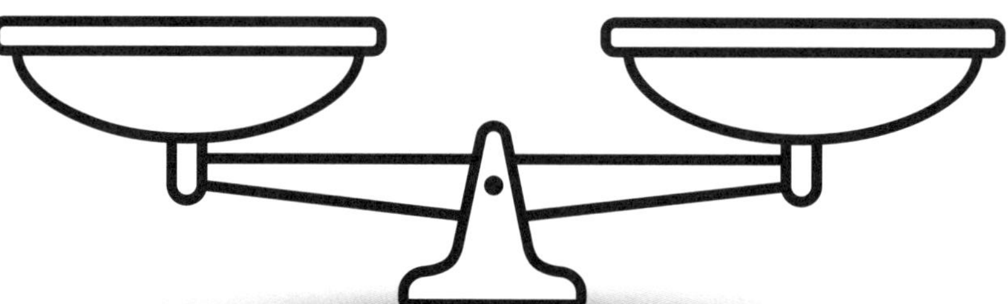

Where can you be more assertive in bringing balance to your relationship?

Use the questions below to reflect on your relationship and determine whether there's a healthy balance of giving, receiving, and mutual respect.

How do we both make an effort to show care and concern for each other's well-being?

How do we both actively contribute to the relationship, ensuring balance so neither feels burdened or neglected?

Is there a balance of accountability where we both take responsibility for our actions?

Are we both equally invested in creating a secure and fulfilling emotional connection?

How are we aligned on fundamental values, goals, and the direction of the relationship?

Observing Balanced Relationships in the World

This practice will help you identify examples of healthy give-and-take dynamics around you and allow you to reflect on how you can incorporate those qualities into your own life.

While you go about your daily life, pay attention to the interactions you notice between people you see. (This can include romantic partners, friends, family members, and strangers).

1. Take note of any balanced exchanges of give and take, shared responsibility, or respectful communication. (Ex: I noticed my friend and her partner share house chores, as one cooks and the other gladly cleans.)
2. Note the behavior or language that stands out to you as healthy and reciprocal. (Ex: I take the trash cans out to the curb, and my partner brings them back in at night.)
3. Note what you want to experience in your relationships based on your observations. (Ex: I want relationships where we consider each other's needs.)
4. Every time you notice a relationship that brings positive feelings of balance, take a moment to feel gratitude for its example. Know that if it's possible for them, it's also possible for you.
5. Repeat affirmations such as "I am worthy of healthy and reciprocal relationships."

By consciously observing and reflecting on balanced relationships, you'll develop a clearer picture of what you want in your connections.

Becoming Interdependent for Secure Partnerships

Interdependency is when we create a healthy balance of depending on others while also depending on ourselves to meet our own physical or emotional needs. Unlike codependency, where we mostly rely on others to meet our needs, or hyper-independency, where we rarely rely on others, interdependency fosters mutual support, trust, and autonomy. Interdependency is a key component to secure partnerships.

How to cultivate interdependency:

Self-Awareness: Become aware of your feelings and the underlying needs (Ex: I am feeling sad and need reassurance that everything will be okay.)

Emotional Regulation: Implement self-soothing techniques (Ex: I can practice box breathing and EFT.)

Meet Your Needs: Identify how you can meet this need yourself before relying on others (Ex: I can practice affirmations such as "I trust that everything will work out as it should," give my "sad part" a hug, and listen to an empowering podcast for motivation.)

Respect Boundaries: If you feel as though external support is necessary, identify how you can be mindful of others' boundaries and needs (Ex: I can ask my friend if she has time to talk with me on the phone tonight and inform her of my needs beforehand.)

The diagram below provides a visual representation of codependent, interdependent, and hyper-independent relationships:

Codependency: You are so entangled with the other person that you lose your sense of self.
Interdependency: You are connected and attuned to each other while maintaining individuality and autonomy.
Hyper-independency: You are together but function as if you're separate.

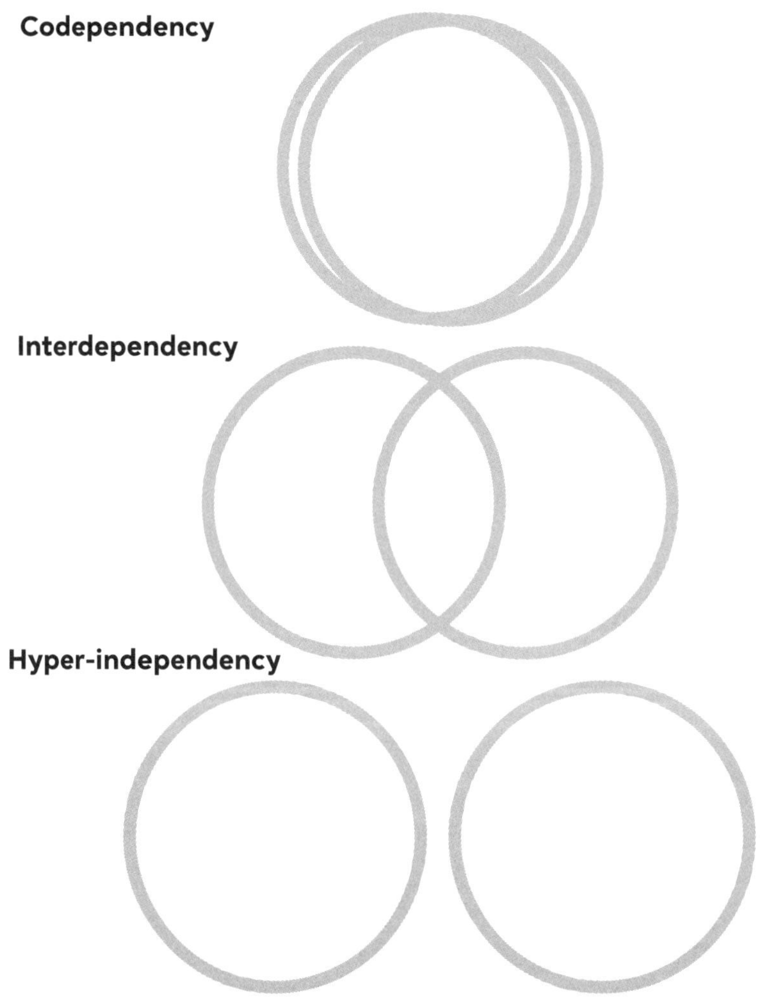

Reflect on your relationships and write about where you feel you are operating from codependency, interdependency, or hyper-independency. Consider:

How do these dynamics show up in your relationships?

What would moving toward a more interdependent dynamic look like for you?

Staying Rooted in Your Self

Becoming a healthy and secure individual requires knowing and being rooted in all the aspects of yourself that make you unique, including your values, beliefs, needs, and boundaries. By becoming aware of these different aspects, you develop a more grounded sense of self, making you less likely to be swayed by your environment or the opinions and behaviors of others. Being rooted in who you are allows you to navigate relationships with confidence and authenticity.

Knowing your relationship values, beliefs, needs, and boundaries is a key component to building healthy connections while maintaining your sense of self in relationships. Fill out the following diagram to clarify these aspects and gain a deeper understanding of what you need to thrive in your relationships.

- My key relationship values (Ex: My values are communication, mutual respect, and togetherness.)
- My key relationship beliefs (Ex: I believe that relationships are a healthy balance of give and take where we support each other's differences and find ways to compromise when needed.)
- My key relationship needs (Ex: I need consistency, predictability, and emotional attunement within my relationships.)
- My key relationship boundaries (Ex: I will not tolerate any form of abuse or mistreatment.)

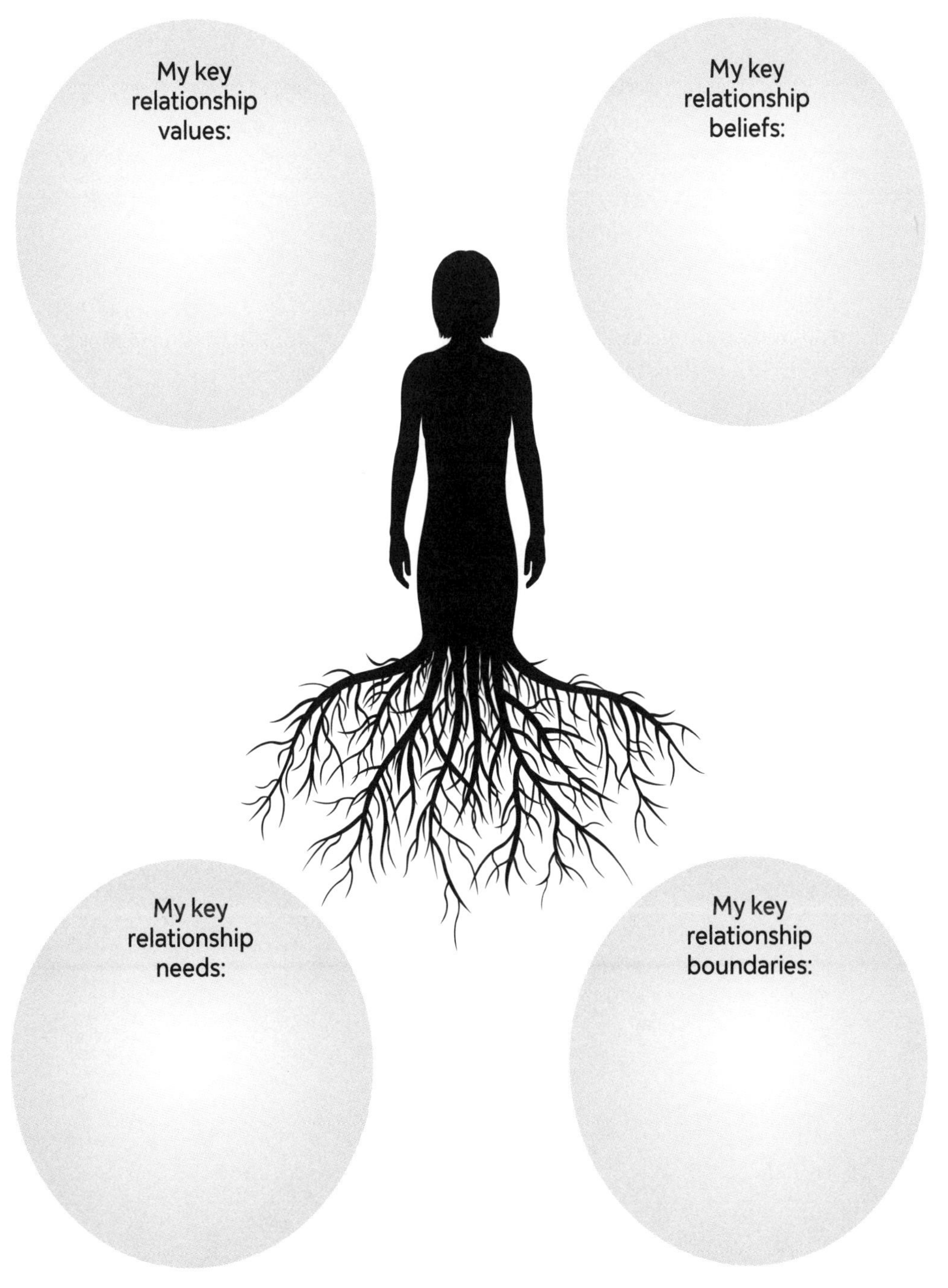
My key relationship values:
My key relationship beliefs:
My key relationship needs:
My key relationship boundaries:

Daily Intention Setting for Breaking Codependency

This simple practice helps you build internal validation, set boundaries, and nurture self-reliance to break codependent patterns.

1. Set a morning intention: (Ex: "I will treat myself to a tasty lunch today and listen to a podcast on self-love.")
2. Ask yourself:
   How do I want my day to go?
   How can I show up for myself and meet these needs?
3. Notice the impulse to over-extend yourself:
4. Throughout the day, when you feel the urge to over-give, over-do, or seek validation, ask yourself:
   What is my intention with doing this thing?
   Am I doing this because I genuinely want to?
   Am I neglecting my own needs to prioritize theirs?
5. Take a step back and re-evaluate your decisions if you notice codependent tendencies.
6. Set boundaries:
   Choose one small boundary to set each day. (Ex: "I will not respond to texts or calls during my morning walk.")
7. Reflect and self-validate:
   At the end of your day, take note of where you set boundaries, tended to your needs, and practiced self-care.
   Tell yourself out loud, "I am proud of you for ________."

A powerful way to stay rooted in your sense of self is by being mindful of the intentions behind your actions. Intentions reflect the "why" behind your decisions, behaviors, or choices, guiding you toward authenticity and purpose. They act as a compass, aligning your actions with your values and aspirations.

Use this space to reflect on your recent actions and answer the following:

- What was my intention behind this action?
- Does this intention align with the interdependent person I want to become?
- If not, how could I adjust my actions to reflect my authentic self more fully?

Key Takeaways

Maintaining your sense of self and practicing interdependency is vital for balanced, healthy relationships. For those with anxious attachment, this self-anchored approach to connection can feel unsettling, as we often equate love with codependency and self-neglect. We've been conditioned to believe relationships are conditional and that we must earn love to feel worthy or have our needs met. However, as discussed in this chapter, neglecting our needs causes us to lose touch with ourselves, leading to burnout and resentment.

Reframing your perception of relationships from codependency to interdependency and taking baby steps every day to align with this version of yourself will help you feel more nourished and fulfilled within yourself and your relationships. It may be hard work initially, but it's worth the effort!

- Relying on self-sufficiency and "doing it all yourself" is unsustainable.
- Understanding your codependent tendencies and learning to break them will help you feel more empowered, confident, and secure in your relationships, as well as more connected to your authentic self.
- Interdependency is required for healthy, secure partnerships.
- Being mindful of your intentions can help you to distinguish what is coming from your codependent self versus your interdependent self.

"I am worthy of love and respect without having to over-give or sacrifice my own needs. I honor myself by setting healthy boundaries and trusting that I can meet my needs while fostering balanced relationships."

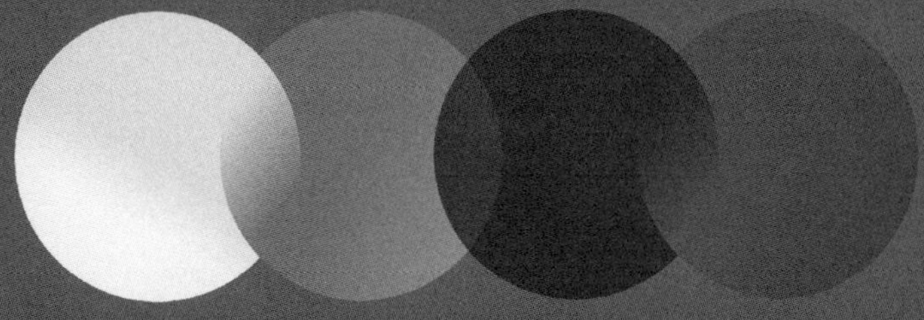

CHAPTER 7

EMBRACING SECURITY IN RELATIONSHIPS

Many people assume they must be fully "healed" before entering a new relationship. However, attachment science shows that true transformation often occurs within relationship dynamics, as we relearn how to experience love and connection in real time. Relationships provide opportunities to practice secure behaviors, communicate needs effectively, and build trust with another person. By learning the tools to navigate relationship challenges and the inevitable phases that follow, we can reshape old attachment patterns and heal.

If you're in a relationship and your partner is open and willing to address their own attachment patterns while doing the necessary work to build a secure bond, this is great news! And if you're single, learning about your attachment patterns now and implementing tools to build a strong foundation of self-awareness and security can help you filter through potential partners more effectively. Not only will this work help you find a compatible match, but it will also equip you with the tools to maintain healthy relationship dynamics once you've established a connection.

In this chapter, you will explore exercises, practices, and prompts designed to help you feel more confident in identifying relationships that complement your attachment needs. You'll also gain the tools to navigate those relationships with clarity and confidence, empowering you to build the secure, fulfilling connections you truly desire.

Breaking the Cycle of Unhealthy Love

Tracy had been single for two years. After a series of tumultuous relationships where her anxious attachment tendencies flared due to the chaos and consistent ups and downs with her partners—many involving different forms of abuse, which she also found herself engaging in—she was hesitant to enter another relationship. She feared repeating the same painful cycles and felt it was safer to remain alone than risk another unhealthy dynamic. Tracy was convinced she was a magnet for emotionally unavailable, narcissistic partners. She struggled to understand why she consistently attracted self-centered individuals who would overwhelm her with affection (also known as "love-bombing"), appear completely infatuated, and then withdraw emotionally once she became invested.

Tracy committed to doing the inner work to understand her patterns and build confidence and security within herself. While much healing can happen independently, true transformation often occurs within the context of relationships. By helping Tracy clarify her needs and recognize what healthy love looks and feels like, she became more attuned to relationships that aligned with her needs. When she eventually encountered a healthy and balanced connection, she was not only able to recognize it but also fully appreciate and nurture it!

"We are born in relationship, we are wounded in relationship, and we can be healed in relationship."

—HARVILLE HENDRIX

Reframing Your Beliefs on Relationships

People with an anxious attachment style often fear repeating the cycle of partnering with emotionally unavailable individuals and being rejected or abandoned by those they love. These fears can lead them to act in ways that feel inauthentic, compromising their true desires and perpetuating insecure relationship patterns.

By challenging these limiting beliefs about relationships, you can reframe them into more supportive and empowering narratives. This shift is a crucial step that motivates you to seek healthy connections and build the secure, fulfilling bonds you truly want to experience.

What are your fears around intimate relationships (platonic and romantic)? (Ex: There are no good people left out there.)

How are these fears limiting your ability to find or create healthy relationships? (Ex: These fears cause me to be highly skeptical and judgmental of all potential love interests.)

How would you approach relationships if you were free of these fears? (Ex: I would be more relaxed and optimistic when meeting new people.)

What's a more empowering belief you can tell yourself to support your true desires? (Ex: There are secure, emotionally available people in the world, and I am open to finding them while being discerning with my choices.)

Creating affirmations aligned with your desired relationship outcomes is a powerful way to build supportive beliefs. Choose affirmations from the list below or create your own, and reflect on how they resonate with you:

- "I am worthy of love, appreciation, and security."
- "It's safe to express my feelings and needs."
- "If someone isn't right for me, I will find someone who is."
- "There are good, secure people in the world."
- "The right people will love me as I am."
- "Healthy relationships are built on respect and support."
- "I am easy to love."

Write your chosen affirmations and how they align with your goals.

How to Find a Compatible Match—Red Flags vs. Green Flags

One of the most common questions I am asked is, "How do I find a compatible partner?" The good news is that attachment theory can help you better filter potential love interests based on what your attachment style needs to feel safe and secure in relationships.

Our relationship needs are rooted in our earliest attachment dynamics. The things we lacked in childhood often become the very things we seek in relationships to cultivate secure attachment. The challenge is that, without awareness of these attachment needs, we tend to invest in relationships that feel familiar but aren't necessarily healthy for us.

It's not that you only attract emotionally unavailable or avoidantly attached individuals—it's that you choose to invest in those relationships. By learning to recognize red flags and green flags, you can better discern potential partners based on their behaviors and how they align with your needs. Remember, it takes time to observe patterns and truly assess compatibility. Be patient and intentional in the process.

Take some time to reflect on and note what these red flags look like to you in real time.

Red Flags

Mixed signals
Lack of emotional support
Insensitive
Rigid
Dismissive
Self-centered
Low patience
Defensive
Avoids commitment
Flakes
Emotionally closed off
Inconsistent

Green Flags

Emotional availability
Open communication
Attentive
Validating
Mutual connections and understanding
Emotionally supportive
Inclusive
Consistent
Reliable
Comfortable with deeper intimacy
Respects boundaries

Shifting Perspectives: Viewing Relationships Through a Secure Lens

As you go about your daily life, practice noticing your thought patterns—whether you're having a conversation, scrolling through social media, reading an article, or listening to a podcast. Many of these interactions can trigger fearful thinking patterns about relationships.

For example:

- Your friend shares that she was cheated on and insists that all men are liars.
- You come across statistics claiming that most people in the dating pool are avoidantly attached.
- You see a post on social media suggesting that your attachment style and your partner's are doomed to fail.

In today's information era, we are constantly bombarded with opinions and data. Depending on your existing belief systems about relationships, you'll unconsciously filter this information in ways that reinforce your fears, keeping you stuck in old, unhelpful patterns.

Instead, imagine looking at the world through a secure lens. How might that transform the information you're exposed to? By reframing what you take in, you can shift your perspective toward more supportive and optimistic narratives.

Your belief systems shape your reality. Choose empowering beliefs by pausing to question fearful thoughts and reframing them through a lens of security and possibility.

People with an anxious attachment style often feel a sense of urgency when searching for potential partners, which can lead to impulsive decisions. To ease this urgency, focus on filling that void by nurturing yourself and building a fulfilling life.

What are the things that truly bring me joy?

______

______

______

______

______

______

Who can I reach out to for support?

______

______

______

______

______

______

Who do I like to spend time with?

______

______

______

______

______

CONTINUED >

CONTINUED FROM THE PREVIOUS PAGE

What activities can I do in my spare time?

How can I get involved in my community?

What projects would I love to start?

Practice doing these things to create space and patience while you date and get to know new people.

When to Stay In or Leave a Relationship?

Let's say you're in a relationship and realize you've been deeply unhappy. You recognize that your dissatisfaction stems from your relationship needs not being met. While you love your partner and have invested so much into the relationship, you're afraid they may not rise to meet your needs.

To help you determine whether to stay or leave, consider asking yourself the following questions:

Do we share similar core values and long-term goals?

Have I clearly communicated my feelings and needs in a proactive manner?

Is my partner open to understanding attachment patterns and learning tools for a secure bond?

Is there mutual effort and consistency in nurturing the relationship?

Is this relationship helping me grow into a secure version of myself?

Am I holding on, hoping they'll change, rather than accepting them as they are?

Has there been real progress in problem areas, or just empty promises?

Is this relationship causing more harm than fulfillment?

Based on how you answered these questions, assess if this relationship is fostering your growth, happiness, and emotional well-being, or if it is draining, unfulfilling, or misaligned with your values and needs. Seek professional support if needed.

Nobody is perfect, including ourselves, which means mistakes will happen in any relationship. When evaluating whether to stay or leave, it's important to take a flexible approach.

Reflect on the following question and write your thoughts below:

Is my partner consistently making an effort to meet my needs, communicate openly, respect my boundaries, and nurture the relationship for the most part?

- Note the inclusion of "for the most part."
- Focus on overall patterns of behavior rather than isolated incidents. Use this space to explore your observations, identify any recurring issues, and consider how these patterns impact your well-being.

Be the Observer and Look for Patterns

Love always carries some risk. While we can't predict how relationships will unfold, we can make informed choices by observing patterns during the dating stage to understand someone more deeply.

Those with anxious attachment often rush into relationships when their needs feel met, but the honeymoon stage can mask true behaviors. Taking time before fully committing or attaching is crucial for self-protection and long-term well-being.

Although refraining from immediate attachment may feel challenging due to a deep desire to find safety and belonging within the bond of a relationship, stepping back and observing is essential.

Allow yourself a few months (three or more) to assess for consistent patterns. As you date, ask yourself the following questions and observe what you see. Remember that we all make mistakes on occasion, so these questions should be focused on your partner's typical behavior.

- Do this person's words align with their actions?
- Are they consistent with their actions?
- Do they make an effort to meet my needs?
- Are they open and responsive when I communicate my feelings and needs?
- Do they take accountability?

Observing these behaviors helps ensure you build relationships based on trust and consistency.

Healing Your Relationship Road Map

Creating a safe and secure relationship requires openness, commitment, and mutual effort. With time and dedication, relationships can heal and thrive, embodying the trust, care, and nurturance we all desire. This exercise offers a step-by-step guide to help you and your loved one strengthen your connection and create a secure bond.

1. Identify key areas for growth: Review the road map below, which outlines essential building blocks for cultivating a secure relationship.
    - Balance meeting needs
    - Communicate clearly
    - Respect boundaries
    - Challenge insecure thinking patterns
2. Choose a focus area: Select one or two areas to concentrate on for the next month.
3. Set actionable goals: Write down specific steps you can take to improve in this area. For example:
    - **To communicate clearly:** Commit to weekly check-ins to share feelings and concerns.
    - **To respect boundaries:** Practice expressing your discomforts clearly and respectfully.
4. Track your progress: Reflect weekly on how you and your loved one are implementing these changes.
5. Shift focus gradually: Once you've built confidence in one area, move to the next, allowing for steady progress toward a more secure and fulfilling relationship.

Use the space below to outline your goals and track your journey.

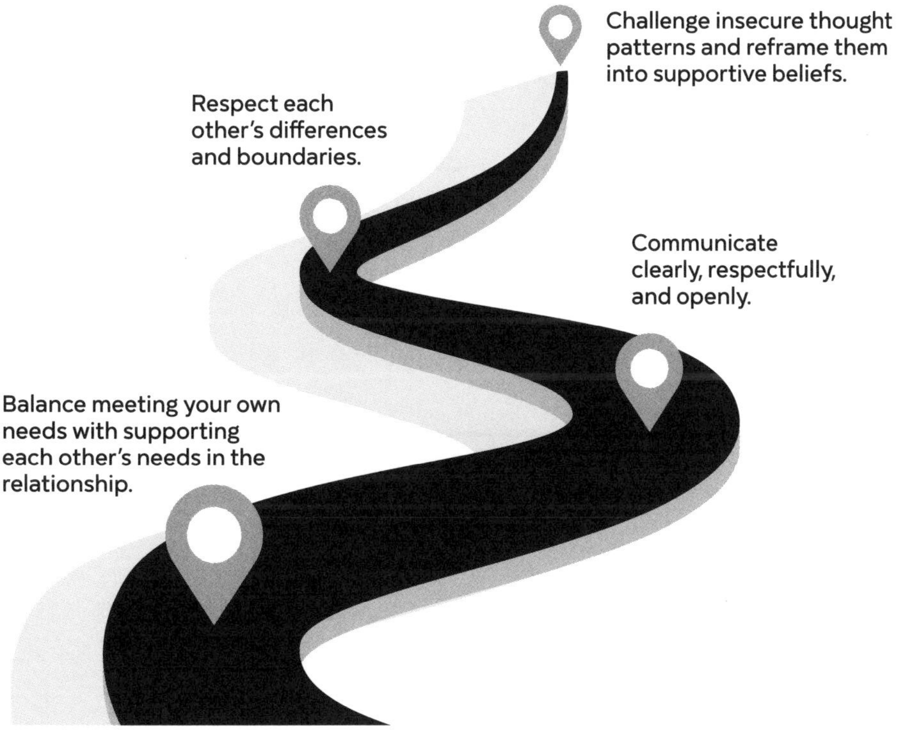

Challenge insecure thought patterns and reframe them into supportive beliefs.

Respect each other's differences and boundaries.

Communicate clearly, respectfully, and openly.

Balance meeting your own needs with supporting each other's needs in the relationship.

Consistency and reliability are the foundation of secure relationships. They involve following through on promises, aligning words with actions, and showing up consistently to build trust and reduce anxiety.

Use the questions below to reflect on how you and your partner practice these qualities.

- Are we both saying what we mean and meaning what we say?
- Are we showing consistency between our words and actions?
- Are we honoring our commitments to each other?
- Are we taking accountability and offering reassurance when we fall short?

Explore areas of strength and opportunities for growth.

Trust That It Will All Work Out

Our beliefs are powerful! As we've discussed throughout this book, they shape our thoughts, feelings, and behaviors. Together, these three components create patterns that influence the reality we experience. If you believe that you will never find love, that you are undeserving of love, or that you can't build a healthy, secure relationship, those beliefs will manifest in your reality. However, if you firmly believe that you are worthy of and capable of experiencing healthy, secure love, your thoughts, feelings, and actions will align to support that outcome.

This process is called the self-fulfilling prophecy—the idea that our beliefs drive the choices and behaviors that ultimately make those beliefs come true. By cultivating empowering and supportive beliefs, you set the foundation for creating the life and relationships you desire.

If you knew with absolute certainty that you would experience a healthy, secure relationship:

What kind of thoughts would you be thinking? (Ex: I trust that what is meant for me will find me at the right time.)

CONTINUED >

CONTINUED FROM THE PREVIOUS PAGE

What kind of feelings would you be experiencing? (Ex: confidence, peace, and joy)

What kind of actions would you take? (Ex: remain open to love and connection)

Moving forward, practice approaching life in this way!

Creating Realistic Expectations in Relationships

To create healthy relationships, whether romantic, familial, or platonic, it's essential to set realistic expectations that honor your needs while accepting each other's differences. This practice encourages flexibility in your relationships, helping you avoid ongoing disappointment and build stronger communication.

1. Identify your relationship needs: Reflect on your most important needs in your relationships. Try to be specific.
2. Create flexible expectations: For each need, think of a flexible way to meet it that considers the other person's individuality. Use the examples below as guidance:

   Attention: Instead of wanting to talk every two hours, agree to check in during key moments (morning, afternoon, evening).

   Reassurance: Instead of constantly seeking verbal affirmations, take note of when they naturally offer reassurance, and revisit those moments when doubt creeps in

   Affection: Instead of immediate connection after time apart, allow them time to decompress before engaging.

   Quality Time: Instead of expecting them to join all your hobbies, find shared activities you both enjoy.
3. Apply and reflect: Practice implementing these flexible expectations and reflect on how they impact your relationships. Would you be able to have a conversation with the other person around these expectations?

This prompt will help you build confidence in finding secure and healthy relationships by shifting from passively waiting for love to actively preparing for it. By identifying actionable steps in the diagram, you'll feel more in control of your journey and reinforce the belief that love is within your reach.

Inside each petal of the flower, write down an activity or goal.

Ideas/Examples:

- Pursue hobbies or passions that fulfill you and bring joy.
- Practice clear communication and expressing your needs with friends or family.
- Reflect on your values and the qualities you seek in a partner.
- Work on self-care routines that boost your confidence and emotional stability.
- Expand your social network.

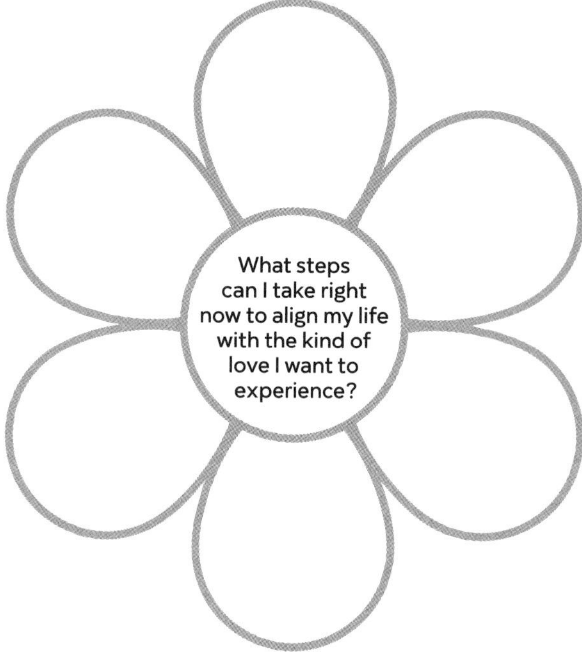

"I am willing and capable of experiencing healthy, secure relationships in my life."

Key Takeaways

Doing the inner work to heal our attachment style, break unhealthy patterns, and build healthier connections is possible for everyone! The best part is that you don't need to be "fully healed" or fully secure to enter into a relationship or improve the one you're already in! All it takes is openness and a willingness to shift your ways of thinking, feeling, and behaving when it comes to matters of the heart to reflect the balanced and mutually supportive relationships you want to experience.

- You can do the work independently to adopt the mindset and behaviors of secure attachment; however, much of your attachment healing occurs within relationships as you relearn how to experience love and connection in a new way.
- Understanding your attachment needs helps you assess compatibility with the people you meet.
- Asking yourself powerful reflective questions can help determine whether to stay in or leave a relationship.
- Insecure relationship patterns can transform into secure connections with mutual effort and support.
- Shifting your beliefs about relationships to be empowering and optimistic can greatly influence your ability to experience healthy, secure love.

CHAPTER 8

THE ROAD AHEAD

Now that you've made it this far, you might be wondering, *Can I maintain these skills? What if I fall back into my old, insecure patterns? What if I fail? Am I doomed?*

These are common concerns for people with insecure attachment styles who are eager to break free from their patterns. However, I want to assure you that once you've gained awareness of this information and, more importantly, begun implementing these skills in your daily life, it becomes increasingly difficult to revert to old unhealthy habits. You now have a new framework and tools to move forward with intention and clarity.

Remember, no one is perfect. We all fall short at times. The key is to show yourself compassion and grace, then choose to respond differently moving forward. Every interaction is an opportunity to practice and strengthen your relationship skills. Be gentle with yourself—progress takes time.

In this chapter, you will learn tools to trust yourself and prioritize self-care. You'll become more confident in making decisions from a place of authenticity rather than fear, and you'll learn how to distinguish between the two. The exercises, practices, and prompts provided will help you create a solid foundation within yourself, allowing you to navigate relationships with trust, security, and resilience.

Breaking Free from Self-Doubt and Embracing Inner Confidence

Drew had been bombarded by self-doubt his entire life. With an anxious attachment style, he was an overthinker who relied heavily on the validation of others to make decisions. As a codependent child who was never encouraged to develop his own sense of identity, Drew struggled to trust his own judgment and inner wisdom.

Through our sessions together, we worked on helping him tune into his inner voice and recognize when his decisions aligned with his true values and desires, rather than being driven by a need for external validation and reassurance.

With time and practice, Drew noticed a growing sense of confidence. He realized that his self-doubt wasn't a reflection of his abilities but a pattern rooted in fear and insecurity. He started making small, independent decisions that allowed him to build trust in his ability to navigate challenges without constantly seeking approval from others. Each step reinforced his confidence and strengthened his connection to his inner wisdom. Eventually, Drew broke free from his excessive dependency on external validation and began living a life guided by his own sense of worth, authenticity, and purpose.

"Follow your instincts. That's where true wisdom manifests itself."

—OPRAH WINFREY

Do You Trust Yourself?

People with an anxious attachment style often struggle with self-trust and rely heavily on others for their sense of self-worth, emotional stability, guidance, and validation. This over-reliance can create unhealthy dynamics, leaving them feeling even more disconnected from themselves and their truth.

Answer "Yes" or "No" to the questions below to assess whether you tend to place more trust in yourself or others when making relationship decisions:
Do I often doubt my decisions and seek reassurance from others?
Yes / No

Do I feel uneasy making decisions without input or validation from others?
Yes / No

Do I immediately turn to others for advice when faced with a challenge?
Yes / No

Do I feel confident in my ability to make choices that align with my values and needs?
Yes / No

Do I trust my intuition?
Yes / No

Do I believe I can handle the consequences of my choices?
Yes / No

Am I able to self-soothe during difficult times?
Yes / No

Do I believe I am capable of learning and growing from my mistakes?
Yes / No

Reflect on your answers to identify patterns in how you approach self-trust. Use this insight to explore how you can strengthen your connection to your inner wisdom.

When making life decisions, it's important to check in with ourselves first and foremost to practice interdependence and make choices that consider our values and needs. Think of a big decision you need to make and use the questions below to explore your motivations and build confidence.

Am I seeking advice because I value this person's perspective or because I doubt my own judgment?

____

____

____

____

____

What would happen if I trusted my instincts and made this decision independently?

____

____

____

____

____

Does this choice bring me closer to the person I want to be and the life I want to create?

____

____

____

____

____

Distinguishing Your Value Systems to Make Well-Informed Decisions for Your Life

In order to begin trusting ourselves, we need to understand and identify our values. Values reflect the things that are most important to us. We can conceptualize them as our core principles that guide our decisions and behaviors. Once identified, we can use them as an internal compass, helping us stay aligned with our authentic selves.

We hold values in all areas of our lives, including romantic relationships, friendships, family, well-being, health, and career. However, those with an anxious attachment style may lack awareness of their own values or feel their values are intertwined with those of others. This can lead to making inauthentic decisions that don't reflect their true needs and desires, often resulting in unfulfilling situations and relationships.

Use the diagram on the following page to become clear on your values so that you can create a foundation for making decisions that honor who you are and what you truly want.

Example:

- **Romantic relationships:** respect, communication, transparency, playfulness
  Friendship: support, trust, authenticity
- **Family:** unity, inclusivity, connection
  Career: growth, creativity, financial security
- **Health:** eating well, working out, consistency
- **Personal well-being:** joy, freedom, novelty

Learn from Your Mistakes

Self-trust comes from relying on your inner wisdom and making choices that align with what you know is best for yourself.

Wisdom comes from reflecting on and learning from your daily experiences—mistakes included! Without reflection, and by consistently relying on others for guidance, you miss the opportunity to build your own internal compass, leaving you more susceptible to the opinions of those around you.

Steps to Build Self-Trust:

1. Make decisions for yourself: When faced with a decision, notice the urge to seek guidance from others. Instead, boldly choose to decide for yourself.
2. Embrace mistakes: Give yourself permission to make mistakes and view them as opportunities for learning rather than failures.
3. Reflect on your choices: After making a decision, ask yourself:

    How did this choice feel for me?

    What did I learn?

    How might I respond differently next time?

    Acknowledge your decisions without judgment and focus on what you can learn from these experiences.
4. Celebrate your wins: Recognize and celebrate moments where you trusted your inner wisdom, no matter how small.
5. Repeat and build confidence: Follow this process consistently, and over time, you'll feel more confident in making decisions that reflect your true self.

While needs are essential for well-being and are required for you to thrive, values are about what you prioritize to live a meaningful and fulfilling life. Needs are nonnegotiable for survival, whereas values are principles that shape priorities and actions.

To best align your decisions with your values, consider the following questions:

What am I feeling? (Ex: I feel anxious and uncertain.)

What do I need to feel better? (Ex: I need clarity and reassurance.)

CONTINUED >

CONTINUED FROM THE PREVIOUS PAGE

How can I align my values to meet my needs? (Ex: If I value support, I'll reach out to someone I trust. If I value self-reliance, I'll reflect first.)

Transforming Comparison into Helpfulness

Those of us with an anxious attachment style have a habit of comparing ourselves to others. We compare our looks, belongings, lifestyles, finances, careers, families, friends, and, of course, our romantic relationships.

Like a double-edged sword, just as comparing can help us identify the things we want to have and experience, it can also cause us to go into a negative spiral of self-deprecation and bitterness.

Use this table to reflect on your comparison habits and shift them into opportunities for growth and alignment with your values. One way we can practice turning comparison into helpfulness is by reflecting on the following questions:

QUESTION	YOUR REFLECTIONS
How might my journey differ from others' in meaningful ways?	
What is it about this person or situation that reflects something I want to create or experience in my own life?	
Instead of focusing on what I lack, what do I already have that supports my strengths and goals?	
Rather than dwelling on comparison, what actions can I take to align myself with my desires?	
Do these desires truly align with my values and the person I want to become?	

By completing this table, you can transform comparisons into insights, helping you focus on your own growth and the life you want to create.

Rather than comparing yourself to the securely attached representations you see around you and believing you'll never measure up to those healthy ways of experiencing relationships, practice using secure attachment as a positive working model. Align your thoughts, feelings, and behaviors with those of secure attachment in your own unique and authentic way.

It's not about pretending to be someone you're not—it's about embodying the mindset, skills, and habits that reflect the healthy, secure relationships you want to create. To begin this process, reflect on this question:

What does a secure relationship mean to me, and what would it look and feel like to experience that?

You Got Yourself

People with an anxious attachment style often struggle to rely on themselves for support, which reinforces their dependency on others for safety and security. While it's perfectly normal and healthy to seek support from others, it's equally important to trust that we can depend on ourselves in moments of loneliness and need.

Connecting to your heart is a simple yet powerful practice to cultivate self-reliance. In moments of discomfort, try the following steps:

1. Pause: Place your hands gently on your heart and close your eyes if you're able to.
2. Breathe: Take slow, deep breaths, feeling your chest expand and contract with each inhale and exhale.
3. Feel the support: Notice the sensation of your hands on your chest, grounding and supporting you. Apply pressure, as if you're physically holding yourself steady. Allow this touch to remind you that you are here for yourself.
4. Self-embrace: Wrap your arms around yourself, giving yourself a comforting hug.
5. Affirm: Repeat to yourself, "I am safe in this moment, and I've got you no matter what." Say it as many times as you need, letting the words sink in.

This practice is a gentle way to reconnect with yourself and cultivate a sense of safety and self-reliance.

Focusing on the Positive

People with an anxious attachment style have a strong negativity bias, meaning they quickly focus on the negative rather than the positive. This mechanism is wired into all humans for survival purposes; however, if we've grown up in environments where getting our needs met was inconsistent or unpredictable, we tend to assume worst-case scenarios.

This can be troublesome for various reasons, including increasing our anxiety and hypervigilant tendencies, and projecting our fears and insecurities onto those we love.

Use the table below to reflect on the positive aspects of your day. This practice helps counteract negativity bias, rewiring your brain to notice uplifting moments and fostering a more balanced perspective.

QUESTION	YOUR REFLECTIONS
What situations worked out in my favor today?	
Who offered help or support today?	
What strengths did I notice in my partner or those around me?	
What affirmations or kind words did I receive?	
What things was I given or did I received today?	
What accomplishments, big or small, can I validate for myself?	
What moments brought me love, joy, or comfort today?	

Reflecting on these questions daily will help you shift your focus from potential threats to positive experiences, creating greater emotional balance and fostering healthier relationships.

What is one specific thing my partner/friend/family member did something that I appreciated?

What qualities in this person do I admire, and how do they add value to my life?

How does this person show care, even in small or subtle ways?

What challenge have we faced together, and how has it strengthened our relationship?

How has this person supported or inspired me to grow?

What do I feel lucky to have in this relationship that I may sometimes take for granted?

Self-Care: Prioritizing Your Self

People with an anxious attachment style tend to equate meaning and purpose with what they can do for others. However, I want to challenge you to begin putting that energy and love into your relationship with yourself. We must prioritize and cultivate a relationship with ourselves, as it's the only relationship we can guarantee will last throughout our lifetime.

Seeking professional support, whether therapy, coaching, or mentoring, can help you cultivate the understanding and skills to strengthen your relationship with yourself and others. One way to achieve this is to do for yourself what you do for others, and be for yourself what you wish others could be for you.

What do I love doing for others? (Ex: Caretaking)

____

____

____

____

____

____

How can I do these things for myself? (Ex: Cook a delicious and thoughtful meal for myself)

____

____

____

____

____

Who do I need others to be for me? (Ex: My emotional support system)

How can I be those things for myself? (Ex: Learn to reassure and validate myself, as well as create a large support system to help me navigate life's challenges)

Gratitude Practice

Another effective way to counter negative thoughts and assumptions is through practicing gratitude. Gratitude has become a widely discussed topic—and for good reason! Research shows that daily gratitude practice can boost happiness, improve psychological well-being, enhance self-esteem, promote better health, and strengthen relationships.

A simple way to incorporate gratitude into your daily life is to wake up each morning and call to mind ten things you are grateful for.
Describe in detail what you are grateful for and why.

For example:

- I am grateful for my health, which allows me to be active with my children.
- I am grateful for my home, which keeps me safe.
- I am grateful for my partner, who provides me with emotional stability and love.
- I am grateful for my vehicle, which takes me to and from locations comfortably and easily.
- I am grateful for my bed, which allows me to sleep comfortably at night.
- I am grateful for the abundance of oxygen that allows me to breathe easily and effortlessly.
- I am grateful for the clean water that quenches my thirst whenever needed.
- I am grateful for the sunshine that brings light and warmth to my life.

Healing is not linear, and neither is the journey to becoming securely attached. The goal isn't to be perfect—it's about doing your best to acknowledge your triggers and patterns and responding in healthier ways. By consistently working to shift these patterns, you begin to form new habits that support the healthy, fulfilling relationships you want to experience.

What have I learned from my mistakes or setbacks, and how can I use those lessons to grow?

What is one thing I've improved on compared to where I was a week, month, or year ago?

How can I show myself grace and compassion while taking steps to improve my circumstances?

Becoming securely attached isn't a linear process, it's a journey with many ups and downs along the way.

Key Takeaways

Becoming securely attached is a journey of self-awareness, growth, and taking action to align your behaviors with the desired outcomes you want to experience. Trusting yourself is crucial so that you can make decisions that complement who you truly are and what you truly want. As anxious attachers, it's pivotal to break free from our hyper-dependent tendencies and learn to listen to our own inner wisdom. The more we trust ourselves and learn from our mistakes, the more confidence we have to navigate any challenge that comes our way. Your relationship with yourself is the foundation for all the relationships you will have, and strengthening it will empower you to build healthier, more fulfilling connections with others.

- Learning to trust yourself is essential for making authentic and well-informed decisions for your life.
- Let your choices be rooted in your values.
- Use comparison as a way to empower you, not devalue you.
- It's not about being perfect. It's about celebrating your progress, learning from your mistakes, and showing yourself compassion through the process.
- Seeking support from therapists, coaches, and mentors can be vital for our growth and healing.

“I strive for progress,
not perfection.”

A FINAL WORD

Congratulations on making it to the end of this workbook! While understanding your attachment challenges is an important first step, the real transformation comes from taking actionable steps to shift your unhealthy patterns. By consistently applying the tools and concepts shared here to your daily life, you'll continue to feel more secure within yourself and your relationships.

This journey is a lifestyle change, transforming how we think, feel, and act in relationships. It reshapes who we're attracted to and how we view connections. By showing up as your authentic self, you create relationships that reflect your true worth.

So much of attachment work involves peeling back the layers of what you once thought was "normal" in relationship dynamics and relearning what it means to experience healthy connections. Be gentle with yourself throughout this process—it may feel like an identity shift as you embrace a new reality and a new version of yourself. Seek support from a professional, such as a licensed therapist or trained coach, as they can help you implement these strategies and step into this new phase of growth.

Remember, you have nothing to lose and everything to gain by being your most authentic, secure self. The right people will love and support your growth, while those who aren't aligned will naturally fall away. Keep moving forward, and return to the tools and insights in this book whenever you need to re-center yourself. This resource will always be here for you as you continue your journey toward security and self-empowerment.

RESOURCES

AUTHOR-PROVIDED

Attachment Coaching with Jessica Da Silva, JessicaDaSilvaCoaching.com—End unhealthy relationship patterns by embracing the mindset and habits of secure attachment.

Let's Talk Attachments Podcast with Jessica Da Silva Instagram—@thejessicadasilva

BOOKS

The Anxious Hearts Guide by Rikki Cloos—Gives you a compassionate look into the anxious attachments emotional and behavioral experiences, how they experience relationships, and how to become more secure.

Anxiously Attached by Jessica Baum, LMHC—Offers transformative tools to understand the anxious attachment style, break unhealthy patterns, build self-worth, and create secure relationships.

The Four Relationship Styles by Dr. Anita Knight Kuhnley—Explains the four attachment styles with relatable attributes, helping you understand your behavior and others' actions shaped by attachment insecurities and coping mechanisms.

Getting the Love You Want by Harville Hendrix, PhD, and Helen LaKelly Hunt, PhD—Offers practical insights and exercises to understand relationships, heal past wounds, and build deeper, more meaningful connections based on trust, empathy, and emotional growth.

How to Be an Adult in Relationships by David Richo—Gives you a deeper understanding of the different relationship needs and the importance of identifying, meeting, and communicating your needs for relationship satisfaction.

Keeping the Love You Find by Harville Hendrix, PhD, and Helen LaKelly Hunt, PhD—Guides readers in understanding their past wounds, breaking dysfunctional patterns that no longer serve them, and building and maintaining relationships they find for long-term satisfaction.

Needy No More by Chris Rackliffe—Encourages you to reframe your perspective on needs, understand their importance in your life, and use them to build more fulfilling, secure relationships.

Nonviolent Communication by Marshall B. Rosenberg, PhD—Teaches compassionate communication, helping you express feelings and needs clearly, resolve conflicts, and build stronger, empathetic connections in relationships.

Wired for Dating by Stan Tatkin, PsyD, MFT—Provides scientific and practical insights into how our brains and attachment styles influence relationships, helping readers build lasting connections from the start.

Women Who Love Too Much by Robin Norwood—Offers valuable guidance for women who struggle with unhealthy relationship patterns and a lack of boundaries and guides them on how to prioritize self-love and healing.

PODCASTS

Jillian on Love with Jillian Turecki—Provides practical advice for understanding and navigating relationships, including finding compatible partners, handling breakups, fostering emotional growth, and building healthier, more meaningful connections.

Love Life with Matthew Hussey—Offers straightforward, no-nonsense advice for navigating relationships and dating, empowering readers with practical insights and actionable strategies for finding healthy love.

Mark Groves Podcast with Mark Groves—Provides deeper insights into love and relationship challenges through conversations with expert guests, offering valuable perspectives and strategies for understanding our thoughts, feelings, and behaviors.

On Attachment with Stephanie Rigg—Takes a closer look at the inner dynamics of each attachment style, offering valuable insights into how they shape behaviors, emotions, and relationship patterns.

The Terri Cole Show with Terri Cole—Understand what boundaries are, how they impact our well-being, and the importance of setting them in our lives to prevent resentment, burn-out, and unfulfilling relationships.

YOUTUBE

Briana MacWilliam—Offers insightful videos on attachment styles, emotional healing, and building secure relationships, combining practical tools with a compassionate, creative approach, including art therapy.

Dr. Kim Sage—Explores the challenges of different attachment styles and how they manifest in our lives and examines how autism, narcissism, and trauma can influence our relational experiences.

Heidi Priebe—Offers a detailed exploration of attachment styles, their challenges, and practical strategies to create self-awareness, healthier relationships, and covers other important relationship topics.

Psych2Go—Makes mental health and psychology accessible to people worldwide by creating engaging, lighthearted animated content that simplifies complex concepts around attachment theory and much more.

REFERENCES

Ainsworth, Mary D. Salter., Mary C. Blehar, Everett Waters, and Sally Wall. *Patterns of Attachment: A Psychological Study of the Strange Situation.* Lawrence Erlbaum Associates, 1978.

Beattie, Melody. *Codependent No More: How to Stop Controlling Others and Start Caring for Yourself.* Revised ed. Harper/Hazelden, 2022.

Beck, Aaron T. *Cognitive Therapy and the Emotional Disorders.* International Universities Press, 1976.

Beck, Judith S. *Cognitive Behavior Therapy, Second Edition: Basics and Beyond.* Guilford Press, 2011.

Bowlby, John. *A Secure Base: Parent-Child Attachment and Healthy Human Development.* Basic Books, 1988.

Brown, Brené. "According to Brené Brown, These Three Tricks Are the Key to Setting Better Boundaries." *Oprah Daily.* December 22, 2021.

Cole, Terri. *Boundary Boss: The Essential Guide to Talk True, Be Seen, and (Finally) Live Free.* Sounds True, 2021.

Germer, Christopher K. *The Mindful Path to Self-Compassion: Freeing Yourself from Destructive Thoughts and Emotions.* Guilford Press, 2009.

Greenberger, Dennis, and Christine A. Padesky. *Mind Over Mood: Change How You Feel by Changing the Way You Think.* Guilford Press, 2015.

Greenberg, Mark T., Dante Cicchetti, and E. Mark Cummings, eds. *Attachment in the Preschool Years: Theory, Research, and Intervention.* University of Chicago Press, 1990.

Hayes, Steven C., Kirk D. Strosahl, and Kelly G. Wilson. *Acceptance and Commitment Therapy: The Process and Practice of Mindful Change.* Guilford Press, 2016.

Heller, Diane Poole. *The Power of Attachment: How to Create Deep and Lasting Intimate Relationships.* Sounds True, 2019.

Hendrix, Harville. *Getting the Love You Want: A Guide for Couples, 20th Anniversary Edition.* Henry Holt & Co., 2007.

Johnson, Sue. *Hold Me Tight: Seven Conversations for a Lifetime of Love.* Little, Brown Spark, 2008.
Karen, Robert. *Becoming Attached: First Relationships and How They Shape Our Capacity to Love.* Warner Books, 1994.
Katie, Byron, and Michael Katz. *I Need Your Love—Is that True? How to Stop Seeking Love, Approval, and Appreciation and Start Finding Them Instead.* Harmony Books, 2005.
Kay, Louise L. *You Can Heal Your Life.* Hay House, 2004.
Levine, Amir, and Rachel Heller. *Attached: The New Science of Adult Attachment and How It Can Help You Find—and Keep—Love.* Penguin Publishing Group, 2012.
Reid, Penny. *Truth or Beard.* Cipher-Naught, 2015.
Richo, David. *How to Be an Adult in Love: Letting Love in Safely and Showing It Recklessly.* Shambhala, 2014.
Rosenberg, Marshall B. *Nonviolent Communication: A Language of Life.* 3rd ed. PuddleDancer Press, 2015.
Schwartz, Richard C., and Martha Sweezy. *Internal Family Systems Therapy.* Guilford Press, 2019.
Sroufe, L. Alan., and June Fleeson. "Attachment and the Construction of Relationships." In W. W. Hartup and Z. Rubin (eds.), *Relationships and Development* (pp. 51-71). Hillsdale, NJ: Lawrence Erlbaum Associates, 1986.
Sroufe, L. Alan., B. Egeland, E. Carlson, and W. A. Collins. *The Development of the Person: The Minnesota Study of Risk and Adaptation from Birth to Adulthood.* Guilford Press, 2005.
Tatkin, Stan. *Wired for Dating: How Understanding Neurobiology and Attachment Style Can Help You Find Your Ideal Mate.* New Harbinger Publications, 2016.
Tawwab, Nedra Glover. *Set Boundaries, Find Peace: A Guide to Reclaiming Yourself.* Penguin Publishing Group, 2021.
Vitale, Joe., and Ihaleakala Hew Len. *Zero Limits: The Secret Hawaiian System for Wealth, Health, Peace, and More.* Wiley, 2007.

INDEX

ACKNOWLEDGMENTS

I'd like to express my gratitude to all the attachment researchers who have paved the way for our understanding of love and relationships—John Bowlby, Mary Ainsworth, Mary Main, and many others. Thank you for conceptualizing these experiences so we can better understand ourselves and others. And thank you to Amir Levine, Diane Poole Heller, and Sue Johnson for offering tools to work through our attachment insecurities.

I also want to acknowledge my graduate professors, whose teachings helped me understand the immense impact our early relationship dynamics have on our current lives. They helped me shed the shame I carried for so long, believing my past defined my future. I now know that this is not true.

Finally, I want to honor my courageous clients who face their insecurities head-on, take bold steps to break their attachment patterns, and embrace their secure selves. You inspire me every day. Thank you for your trust, vulnerability, and commitment to growth.

ABOUT THE AUTHOR

Jessica Da Silva, a licensed mental health therapist and attachment coach known for her "What Would Secure Me Do?"® approach, is dedicated to helping adults overcome unhealthy relationship patterns and build secure attachment habits.

As the eldest child of a single immigrant mother, Jessica took on a caretaker role early in life, leading to codependency and anxious attachment tendencies. Discovering attachment theory became a turning point, allowing her to identify and heal dysfunctional relationship patterns.

Jessica holds a BA in psychology from the University of Hawai'i at Mānoa and a master's in counseling from California State University, Los Angeles. She pursued advanced training in life coaching, Neuro-Linguistic Programming (NLP), Emotional Freedom Technique (EFT), and hypnosis to support adults in reconnecting to their authentic selves and fostering healthier relationships.

Through her social media platforms, podcast, coaching, and courses, Jessica has helped thousands worldwide transform their approach to love using practical, evidence-based strategies.

NOTES

NOTES

NOTES